A MESSENGER OF GRACE

A MESSENGER OF GRACE

A study of the life and thought of Abraham Booth

RAYMOND ARTHUR COPPENGER

joshua
press

Josh
press

Joshua Press Inc.
Ontario, Canada
www.joshuapress.com

Distributed by
Sola Scriptura Ministries International
www.sola-scriptura.ca

First Joshua Press edition 2009

© 2009 by Joshua Press Inc.
Editorial director: Michael A.G. Haykin
Book and cover design by Adam Reynolds
Proofreading by Victoria J. Haykin
Typeset in Arno Pro, Interstate, and Chaparral Pro

Library and Archives Canada Cataloguing in Publication available

ISBN-13 978-1-894400-31-2

PRINTED IN THE U.S.A.

To my dear wife, Agnes

"Would I describe a preacher, such as Paul,
Were he on earth, would hear, approve, and own,
Paul should himself direct me. I would trace
His master strokes, and draw from his design.
I would express him simple, grave, sincere;
In doctrine uncorrupt; in language plain,
And plain in manner; decent, solemn, chaste
And natural in gesture; much impressed
Himself, as conscious of his awful charge,
And anxious mainly that the flock he feeds
May feel it too; affectionate in look,
And tender in address, as well becomes
A messenger of grace to guilty men."

WILLIAM COWPER, THE TASK, BOOK II, LINES 395–407

TABLE OF CONTENTS

Foreword   [ix]

Preface   [xi]

Acknowledgments   [xiii]

Chronology   [xv]

Introduction   [xix]

1   England in the time of Abraham Booth   [1]

2   Abraham Booth's early life   [19]

3   The pastorate of the Little Prescott Street Baptist Church   [33]

4   The great religious and social movements of his time   [55]

5   Booth the Calvinist   [77]

6   Communion and baptism   [103]

7   Summary and estimate   [121]

Appendix I: Booth's miscellaneous theological writings   [137]

Appendix II: The complete works of Abraham Booth   [151]

Bibliography   [161]

Biographical sketch   [179]

In his day, and for many years after his death, Abraham Booth was regarded as one of the leading Baptist theologians and thinkers of the eighteenth century. In 1808, two years after Booth had died, Andrew Fuller (1754–1815), the Baptist theologian who was no mean judge of character and thought, publicly praised Booth as "the first counselor of our denomination."[1] Earlier, while Booth was still living, Benjamin Beddome (1717–1795), one of the most significant Baptist hymnwriters of the era, could even exclaim, "Oh, that Abraham Booth's God may be my God."[2] And yet, compared to other key Baptist authors of that period—Fuller and John Gill (1697–1771), for example— relatively little has been done to explore Booth's legacy. Three pieces appeared soon after Booth's death, one by that consummate historical aficionado John Rippon (1751–1836).[3] And in the late 1820s, William Newman (1773–1835), the first president of Stepney Academy, planned a substantial work that never materialized.[4] The next major work did not appear until the mid-twentieth century and it is the work that you hold in your hands.

Raymond Arthur Coppenger was blessed in going to the University of Edinburgh at a time when some exciting new work was being done in Baptist studies there. R.E. Seymour completed a thesis on John Gill the year following the submission of Dr. Coppenger's thesis,[5] and in 1956, A.H. Kirkby submitted his work on Andrew Fuller.[6] Of this trio of studies, Dr. Coppenger's has best withstood the test of time and it is with distinct pleasure that I heartily commend it to the reader as a very fine overview of a key figure in Baptist life in the final decades of the

---

1   Cited Ernest A. Payne, "Abraham Booth, 1734–1806", *The Baptist Quarterly*, 26 (1975– 1976), 28.

2   Cited John Rippon, *A Short Memoir of the Rev. Abraham Booth in James Dore, A Sermon, occasioned by the Death of The Rev. Abraham Booth, Preached in Little Prescott Street, Goodman's Fields…: And A Short Memoir of the Deceased, incorporated with The Address Delivered at his Interment… by John Rippon* (London, 1806), 85, n.*.

3   Rippon, *A Short Memoir of the Rev. Abraham Booth* (1806); William Jones, *Essay on the Life and Writings of the Rev. Abraham Booth* (Liverpool, 1808); and an anonymous "Memoir of the Author" (1813; *Works*, 1:xvii–lxxx).

4   Letter to a son of Abraham Booth, February 17, 1827 (copy in the possession of R.A. Coppenger).

5   "John Gill, Baptist Theologian" (unpublished Ph.D. thesis, University of Edinburgh, 1954).

6   "The Theology of Andrew Fuller and its Relation to Calvinism" (unpublished Ph.D. thesis, University of Edinburgh, 1956).

eighteenth century.

I first came into contact with Dr. Coppenger's work in the 1990s when I was studying Booth's powerful response to the British slave trade. Somewhat later, in 1998, I met his son, Dr. Mark Coppenger— now a dear colleague at Southern Baptist Theological Seminary, then the president of Midwestern Baptist Theological Seminary. I did not immediately make the connection between the two men until Mark told me of his father and his thesis on Booth. And what a delight and privilege it was for me to be introduced to Dr. Ray Coppenger by Mark a year or so ago at the graduation of Dr. Coppenger's grandson, Jedidiah, from Southern in May 2008.

Booth's theological perspectives, particularly with regard to ecclesiology and soteriology, need to be studied afresh at the beginning of the twenty–first century, and I can think of no better place to begin the study of this mentor than this book by Dr. Coppenger. May God use it for his glory!

Michael A.G. Haykin
The Southern Baptist Theological Seminary
Louisville, Kentucky
August 2009

When my sister Anne and I were preschoolers, our father, Raymond Arthur Coppenger, was a professor at Belmont College in Nashville, Tennessee. He was just finishing his dissertation, begun several years earlier in Edinburgh. Our mother, Agnes, who had walked with him through years of study, both in Scotland and America, did much of the typing. I had no idea what he was writing about and that I would one day come to cherish Booth's perspectives: Little did I know that, as a faculty member at The Southern Baptist Theological Seminary (my father's alma mater), I would affirm the doctrines of grace; that, as a pastor in Arkansas and Illinois, I would baptize converts who had been sprinkled as infants; that, as an editor of *Kairos Journal*, I would help publish some of Booth's anti-slavery preaching.

As I write this, my father is about to turn 100 years old, and he continues to bless the body of Christ. He is a cherished member of First Baptist Church, Arkadelphia, Arkansas, and an emeritus professor of Ouachita Baptist University. Though he comes from humble beginnings, the son of a hewer of railroad ties in east Tennessee, he has distinguished himself as a Renaissance man—as a naval chaplain in the Pacific in WWII; as a home builder and auto-mechanic (making the most of a professor's and supply-preacher's income); as a tennis coach, a tour leader, and a quartet bass. Above all, he has been a conspicuous and faithful servant of the Lord, an inspiration and guide for his family and colleagues.

It is a particular joy, then, to see this dissertation in print, because I love and admire my father, and because his writing lifts up the life and work of Abraham Booth, to whom we Baptist pastors owe a great debt.

I would like to thank Dr. Michael Haykin, who has taken a special interest in my father's work on Booth. He and his colleague at Joshua Press, Heinz Dschankilic, have been a great encouragement to us both. Thanks, also, to Southern Seminary's Media Services shop and Evanston Baptist Church's Mike Blissett for moving the dissertation from typescript to digital format.

Mark Coppenger
The Southern Baptist Theological Seminary
Louisville, Kentucky

ACKNOWLEDGMENTS

Research for this thesis has taken the author to most of the places associated with Abraham Booth and necessitated many inquiries in those places relative to locations, descendants, and manuscript materials. To all who so generously assisted, I again express my thanks.

Perhaps the number of libraries visited in search of materials may appear out of proportion to the findings, but I want here to express my appreciation to the librarians and staff members for every assistance and cooperation. The following are the libraries searched: New College, Old College, Edinburgh City Library, National Library of Scotland, The John Ryland Library, Baptist Union Library, British Museum Library, Regent's Park College, Bodleian, Bristol Baptist College, National Library of Wales, National Library of Belgium, and the National Library of Holland.

In America, the following libraries have been visited and have been of inestimable service: Cumberland University, Southern Baptist Theological Seminary, Vanderbilt University, Peabody College, Scarritt College, Fisk University, and Southern Baptist Historical Society Repository. Through interlibrary loan the following libraries have been of inestimable service: Colgate-Rochester Divinity School, William Jewell College, American Baptist Historical Society Collection, and the Library of Congress have supplied many materials.

I here express my deep gratitude to my advisors, the Rev. Principal Hugh Watt and Rev. Dr. Charles S. Duthie. Rev. J.B. Primrose and Miss E.R. Leslie were unfailing in their help in the New College Library. I thank Dr. E.A. Payne, Secretary of the Baptist Union of Great Britain and Ireland, who made available his collection of manuscript letters and Miss Joyce Booth who transcribed these letters after the loss of my first set of notes. Mr. A.J. Raper, Secretary of the Church Hill Baptist Church, Walthamstow, helped greatly by making available the Minute Books of the Little Prescott Street Baptist Church. Dr. Leo Crismon, Librarian of the Southern Baptist Theological Seminary, and Dr. Edward C. Starr, Curator of the American Baptist Historical Collection, have given invaluable assistance, as have Misses Ruth Randle and Nettie Dillard of Cumberland University. Mr. Peter de Visser, General Manager of the William B. Eerdmans Publishing Company, furnished an extensive file of reviews of the 1949 edition of Abraham Booth's *Reign of Grace*. My gratitude I express also to Dr. H.C. Witherington of Belmont College and Professor E.C. Rust of Southern Baptist Theological Seminary, for much friendly counsel and advice. I thank my family for their love and patience throughout the work, most of all my wife, for her assistance and for her preparation of the finished typescript.

R.A. Coppenger
Edinburgh, Scotland
and Nashville, Tennessee, U.S.A.
1953

CHRONOLOGY

1734	Born May 20
1750	Became a stocking weaver
1755	Baptized as a General Baptist
1758	Married Elizabeth Bowmar
1758	Opened school at Sutton-Ashfield
1758–1760	*On Absolute Predestination*
1760	Superintendent of General Baptist work, Kirkby-Woodhouse
1763–1764	Became a Particular Baptist
1765	Began Particular Baptist preaching at Bore's Hall, Sutton-Ashfield
1768	Published *The Reign of Grace*
1768	Called to Little Prescott Street Baptist Church, London
1769	Ordained February 16, Little Prescott Street, London
1770	*The Death of Legal Hope*
1771	Joined the Baptist Board of London Ministers
1772	*The Christian Triumph*
1772	Gave *Address at Interment* of Ann Williams
1775	Organized Prayer and Alms Society

1775   Proposes organization of Sunday School at
        Little Prescott Street

1776   Gave *Address at Interment* of Thomas Wilton

1777   *The Deity of Jesus Christ*

1778   *Apology for the Baptists*

1782   Gave *Address at Interment* of Benjamin Wallin

1782   Daughter church of Little Prescott Street organized
        at Preston

1784   *Paedobaptism Examined*

1786   Gave *Address at Interment* of Samuel Gill

1788   *Essay on the Kingdom of Christ*

1792   *Defence of Paedobaptism Examined*

1792   *Commerce in the Human Species*

1792   Recommended John Thomas, first appointee of The
        Baptist Missionary Society

1795   Gave *Address at Interment* of Samuel Stennett

1795   *The Principles of AntiPaedobaptism, and the Practice of
        Female Communion Completely Consistent*

1796   Gave *Address at Interment* of Joseph Swain

1796   *Glad Tidings to Perishing Sinners*

1797   Revised and republished Samuel Wilson's
        Scripture Manual

1797   Led organization of The Society for
Itinerant Preaching

1798   Sunday School organized at Little Prescott
Street Church

1799   Valedictory to first Missionary reinforcements

1800   *Amen to Social Prayer*

1801   Employed assistant pastor, Thomas Coles

1802   Employed assistant pastor, William Gray

1803   *Divine Justice Essential to Divine Character*

1803   Little Prescott Street Sunday School joined Sunday
School Union

1804   Led organization of the Education Society

1805   *Pastoral Cautions*

1806   Died January 27

1813   *Three Essays* posthumously published in
collected works

       1. "On the Love of God to His Chosen People"

       2. "On a Conduct and Character Formed Under the
Influence of Divine Truth"

       3. "Evidences of Faith in Jesus Christ both Negatively
and Positively Considered"

1813   *Thoughts on Dr. Edward Williams' Hypothesis Relative
to the Origin of Moral Evil* (Published posthumously
with collected works)

A young Abraham Booth

[From a sketch by Hélène Grondines ©2009]

INTRODUCTION

The purpose of this thesis is to rediscover and consider an almost forgotten Baptist minister, Abraham Booth (1734–1806), who, through his character, his writings, his influence in moderating the hyper-Calvinism of the Particular Baptists, and his leading part in denominational affairs, must be acknowledged as an important contributor to the spiritual awakening in England. The lines of his thought are safe guides today, and his prodigious work is still an inspiration.

A search in the libraries of the University of Edinburgh and a study of the catalogues of other libraries revealed a few basic materials and showed further that nothing had been written about Booth apart from brief introductions to some of his works, a short memoir, and an essay on his life and writings that appeared immediately following his death. One of his works has been published in more than forty editions, the latest being another American edition. An introductory essay by Thomas Chalmers, praising one of the works of Mr. Booth was called to the author's attention by Dr. Hugh Watt. Such high regard evidenced by the eminent Dr. Chalmers, suggested the probable value of further study of Abraham Booth. For these reasons and also from a desire to know more about the work of the Baptists in the time of England's great revival, this subject was selected.

Some primary sources are: the collected works of Booth, the Church Minute Books of the Little Prescott Street Baptist Church,[1] the Baptist Board Minute Books, and a few manuscript letters. Other sources are: published letters, journals, diaries, biographies, periodicals, general church history materials, and Baptist church histories.[2] Such biographical data are used as may account for the course of Booth's religious development, but the primary intent is analytical rather than biographical.

---

1   This oldest of London's Baptist churches moved from Prescott Street to Commercial Street, and is now six miles north of its original location, in Walthamstow, and is called Church Hill Baptist Church.

2   The writer first read and transcribed notes from many primary sources, but suffered the misfortune of having a case containing most of the notes, stolen from a railroad station in Southampton, on his journey home. It has been necessary, therefore, in replacing the notes, to work from published copies of some of the manuscript material, American publications, and a considerable number of American editions of English works.

Evidence is presented in this thesis to show how considerably the thought and work of Abraham Booth pioneered in tempering high Calvinism with evangelical zeal and so contributed to a spiritual revival among the Baptists of England towards the end of the eighteenth century. His positive encouragement aided in the formation of plans and agencies through which the denomination evangelized and educated many of "the heathen" both at home and in foreign lands. References indicate that his thought influenced Adoniram Judson, originally an American Congregational missionary, who came to a different understanding of baptism on his way to India. Judson became the first American Baptist foreign missionary and was responsible for the organization of a Baptist foreign mission board in America.

A secondary thesis will be recognized to show the remarkable accomplishment of Booth, a man without formal education—less than six months by his own word—rising by rigid self-discipline, application, and the grace of God, to eminence as a dissenting minister, theologian, author, and great-visioned leader of an important segment of the religious world.

An effort is made to trace the development of his thought from his original Arminian position, to the full development of his moderate Calvinism, in all of its applications.

Following a general look at eighteenth-century England and the religious background of the time, Booth's record of service will be examined, representative portions of his published thought will be presented, and his impact upon his own generation and those succeeding will be estimated.

Material for this study has been relatively scarce and fragmentary in nature, but it is sufficient in quantity and importance for the writer to hope that in this dissertation, the work and person of Abraham Booth may regain some of the lustre it bore in his own time.

London in the eighteenth century

1

ENGLAND IN THE TIME
OF ABRAHAM BOOTH

The Revolution of 1688, with all of its attendant influences, should have released an army of forces that would have transformed every area of English life, making for great progress, social and spiritual, and for economic prosperity during the eighteenth century. Such a transformation was not the case, however.

The rigid discipline and strict morality of the Commonwealth period was followed by a strong reaction against things Puritanical. The court of Charles II (1660–1685) set the tempo for immorality and intrigue which continued unabated throughout the reign of James II (1685–1688). The coming of William and Mary (1689–1702) to the throne and the reign of Queen Anne (1702–1714) during the early years of the eighteenth century, brought a little more order and decency to the court, but the masses continued to react against anything reminiscent of Puritanism.

The era introduced by the House of Hanover, in 1714, saw, under George I and George II, a resurgence of immorality and privilege at court which rivalled the worst of the previous century. Thus, the condition commenced so many years before of a monarchy answerable to itself and morally heedless, carried over into a period which should have been marked by a sense of royal responsibility and by a new dignity on the part of the populace. Contrary to the logical expectation, the moral and spiritual life of England reached its lowest level. "The violent reaction against the reign of the Saints continued with more or less force almost to the end of the eighteenth century."[1]

Despite the new Parliamentary power of the people, living conditions continued to show a distressing disparity between classes. The luxury and waste among the relatively few at the top was in marked contrast with the brutal poverty of those at the bottom of the scale. In between there was a slowly growing middle class of tradesmen and manufacturers. Bad treaties, wanton waste, large military establishments, and poor harvests were among the factors that contributed to the poverty of the English people during the eighteenth-century.[2] Sheer necessity forced many poor souls to choose between starvation and stealing.[3] Records exist of the hanging even of children eleven and twelve years old for petty thievery. Other forms of punishment and execution were banishment, beheading, whipping, and being "drawn and quartered." The crime against property, which accounted for more arrests and more imprisonments than all others, was debt.[4]

Other symptoms of social illness were a cheap and tawdry literature,[5] and a theatre that degraded rather than ennobled those who frequented it.[6] Public lotteries had spread to all classes the already absorbing passion for all forms of gambling,[7] while the baiting of animals and cockfighting catered to the low and brutal tastes which characterized the time.

The evil which probably caused more distress and suffering than all others, however, was the excessive drinking of spirits, beer, and gin. The government of the Revolution threw open the trade of distilling to all its subjects upon payment of certain fees and in 1689 forbade importation of spirits from all foreign countries. Lecky saw this move to be of greater significance than any purely political or military event in the eighteenth century, because of its far-reaching consequences. "The fatal passion for drink was at once, and irrevocably, planted in

---

1   Charles J. Abbey and John H. Overton, *The English Church in the Eighteenth Century* (London: Longman's, Green, and Co., 1887 and 1902), 232.

2   James E. Thorold Rogers, *Six Centuries of Work and Wages: the History of English Labor* (London: Swan Sonnenschein and Co., 1908), 468 ff.

3   Robert F. Wearmouth, *Methodism and the Common People of the Eighteenth Century* (London: Epworth Press, 1945), 91.

4   W.E.H. Lecky, *A History of England in the Eighteenth Century* (London: Longmans, Green and Co., 1892), 7:334.

5   Francis Jeffrey, "Miss Edgeworth", *Contributions to the Edinburgh Review*, 656.

6   W.C. Sydney, *England and the English in the Eighteenth Century* (London: Ward and Downey, 1891), 1:165.

7   Lecky, *History of England*, 2:155.

the nation." In the light of this condition, the statement of London physicians in 1750 is understandable, that there were in and about the metropolis no less than 14,000 cases of illness, most of them beyond the reach of medicine, directly attributable to gin.[8] Bishop Benson of Gloucester, writing to Bishop Berkeley from London on February 18, 1752, said:

> Our people are now become—what they never before were—cruel and inhuman. Those accursed spiritous liquors which, to the shame of our Government, are so easily to be had, and in such quantities drunk, have changed the very nature of our people. And they will, if continued to be drunk, destroy the very race of the people themselves.[9]

One of the darkest word-pictures describing the period was given by John Wesley in a pamphlet first published in 1745, entitled, "A Word in Season; or, Advice to an Englishman." In this he said:

> …what wickedness is there under heaven, which is not found among us at this day? Not to insist on Sabbath-breaking in every corner of our land; the thefts, cheating, fraud, extortion; the injustice, violence, oppression, and dissimilation; the lying; the robberies, sodomies, the murders; which with a thousand unnamed villanies, are common to us and our neighbor Christians of Holland, France, and Germany; consider over and above what a plentiful harvest we have of wickedness almost peculiar to ourselves.[10]

Wesley goes on to condemn the foppishness and sloth of the English gentry, the drunkenness and cursing to be found in the streets, and the desertion of the gospel for unholy Deism by great and humble alike.[11]

Their new power and freedom, won through almost a century of revolution, had still not benefited the people in a tangible way. Reaction against the excesses of the rebellious French, and a deep-seated tradition of subservience to the privileged classes, postponed the rise in economic and moral standards so woefully needed by the common citizen.

With those glimpses at the economic, moral, and social conditions

---

8   Lecky, *History of England*, 2:101, 103.
9   Sydney, *England and the English*, 1:62–63.
10   John Wesley, *The Works of the Rev. John Wesley, A.M., Sometime Fellow of Lincoln College, Oxford* (London: Wesleyan-Methodist Book-Room, 1831), 11:183–184.
11   Wesley, *Works*, 11:183–184.

of the day, we will turn to a closer study of the religious conditions that reflect their eighteenth-century setting, which explain in part, the low level of almost all aspects of national life. Two main groups shared the responsibility for religious thought and activity of the time: the Church of England, with its Methodist Societies, and the Dissenters, composed of Presbyterians, Independents, and Baptists. We shall consider first the Established Church, as it was by far the stronger group numerically and politically.

THE CHURCH OF ENGLAND

Religion and politics joined hand in hand in the "Bloodless Revolution," with the Episcopacy experiencing an upheaval and restoration that paralleled that of the monarchy. Under Charles I (1625–1649), Archbishop Laud so provoked Parliament with his insistence on the divine right of kings and bishops that the revolution was precipitated, "which swept away both the king and the bishops, and paved the way for the common man to declare his mind on religious questions." Laud could not foresee that the persecution which he led against the Puritans within the State Church, would eventuate in State-Presbyterianism, their Calvinism gaining strength in opposition to his Arminianism, and their Presbyterianism rebelling against the divine right of bishops.[12]

An attempt at real religious toleration was made under the Commonwealth, when the Independents, who numbered Oliver Cromwell among their ranks, objected to the persecutions imposed by the Presbyterians, now the Established party.[13] The Restoration, however, saw the reestablishment of the Episcopacy and the imposition of the Clarendon Code, a new surge of clerical tyranny, which sought to drive the Presbyterians out of the Church. The Code consisted of a series of acts bearing heavily on all of the Dissenters as well as the Puritans remaining within the English Church. The Corporation Act of 1661 deprived Protestant Dissenters of all share in municipal life, while the Act of Uniformity of 1662 drove out of the State Church all those with Puritan leanings (thereby imparting respectability to Dissent by the addition of the Presbyterians). The Conventicle Act of 1664 and

---

12 A.C. Underwood, *A History of the English Baptists* (London: Kingsgate Press, 1947), 62–63.
13 G.H. Orchard, *A History of the Baptists in England*, ed. J.R. Graves (Nashville: Southwestern Publishing House, 1860), 2:293.

the Five Mile Act of 1665 struck at the worship services and clergy of the Dissenting sentiment.[14]

Parliament succeeded in reinforcing the power of the Episcopacy, despite the efforts of Charles II and James II to use religious toleration as a political weapon. The Test Act of 1673 required anyone who held civil or military office to take a loyalty oath, partake of the sacrament in a parish church, and deny the doctrine of transubstantiation. Aimed primarily at the Romanists, it legislated against Dissenters as well.[15]

The Toleration Act of 1689, following immediately upon the close of the Revolution, served as a compromise, assuring the State Church its privileges, while relieving Dissenters of persecution. The latter were still disqualified from office, but were no longer classed as criminals or deprived of any semblance of religious liberty.[16]

When William III came to the throne, he demanded an oath of allegiance from the clergy. Four hundred of the most sincere churchmen, including seven bishops with the Archbishop of Canterbury at their head and many theologians, refused to sign. This forced the Non-Jurors out of the church, leaving it greatly weakened. The Occasional Conformity Bill of 1711, under the reign of Queen Anne, was another effort to solidify the power of the Church of England by striking at any Dissenter who sought to qualify for civil office by partaking of the sacrament at a State Church just prior to the election.[17]

Although the king ceased to be the spiritual head of the Church in 1688, he continued to exert his influence upon it through appointments and the shaping of its policy. In an age when ambitious men were consumed with a passion for preferment and knew that their only hope lay in standing well at court, it was inevitable that the clergy should curry royal favour.

When church and state become too intimately bound together, the welfare of one becomes the welfare of the other. The result is rarely the spiritualizing of the state but almost always the secularizing and weakening of the church. From 1688 to 1714, a man could not be elected to Parliament who opposed the Church, and the Church, as a consequence, became a political instrument. Canon Overton describes the Church of England as:

---

14 Underwood, *English Baptists*, 96–97.
15 Underwood, *English Baptists*, 104.
16 Underwood, *English Baptists*, 116.
17 Underwood, *English Baptists*, 118.

…an immense engine of political power. The most able and popular statesman could not afford to dispense with her aid. The bench of bishops formed so compact a phalanx in the Upper House of the Legislature, and the clergy could and did influence so many elections into the Lower House, that the church had necessarily to be courted and favored, often to the great detriment of her spiritual character.[18]

Despite the defeats it had suffered during the era just closing, the Church of England seemed to stand, early in the eighteenth century, on the threshold of renewed usefulness and prosperity. The monarch, Parliament, and the people were enthusiastic in her support, but the promising days under "Good Queen Anne" were short-lived.[19] The Schism Act of 1714, which was meant to strike at the root of dissent by making all education subject to license by the Church,[20] lost its sting by the Queen's death on the day it was to became law.

Politically, the Church of England was a power to be reckoned with, but individually, the clergy, with the exception of the outstanding rectors in the towns, were in a precarious position socially and economically. A system of multiple beneficences became an unfortunate necessity to provide a living for these men who often eked out their incomes with menial secular work or as private chaplains, which amounted to little more than a servant's role. Their poverty also led to marriages with rich widows or cast-off mistresses, lowering further the dignity of the Church.[21]

The differentiation, "High Church" and "Low Church" arose during the reign of Queen Anne, as a result of increasingly conflicting theological opinions. The two schools of thought, existing side by side, served to paralyze the Church's political action to the extent that it could not overthrow the religious settlement of the Revolution, which was greatly in danger, until the advent of the Hanoverians.[22]

With the coming of George I (1714–1727) and the Whigs to power, a new influence weakened the Church in a surprising way. The government's stated policy of peace and quiet at any price, served to dampen what spiritual fire remained and prompted Canon

---

18 Abbey and Overton, *English Church*, 282.

19 J.H. Overton, *The Church in England* (London: Gardner, Darton and Co., 1897), 2:210.

20 Duncan Coomer, *English Dissent Under the Early Hanoverians* (London: The Epworth Press, 1946), 5.

21 Lecky, *History of England*, 1:93–98.

22 Lecky, *History of England*, 1:109–112.

Overton's comment, "The rapid change from activity to lethargy which commenced with the accession of George I is one of the most remarkable phenomena in the history of the English Church."[23]

Although the social practices of the day were predominantly base and worldly, there existed side by side with such conditions an absorption in theological controversy. Villages competed in argumentation and "theology was not the preserve of the professional—it was part of the very fabric of the nation's life and everyone thought that he was entitled to express his views."[24] Bishops and clergy often diverted their energies from the proper exercise of their duties to efforts to prove the totally rational character of Christianity, divesting it of all but its moral teachings. The doubts raised by these controversies, which had been multiplying upon themselves since before the Act of Toleration, unsettled even the more earnest minds and provided a convenient excuse for many to avoid the disciplines of the Christian life.[25]

Deism, which might well include all of the arguments of the day, Overton defines as "an acceptance of religion, and even of the Christian religion, without the acceptance of revealed truth as found in Holy Scripture."[26] A Semi-Arianism had begun to spread among the moderate Puritans, the General Baptists, and the Anglo-Catholic section of the Church. The Arian doctrine placed Christ subordinate to the Father, not including him in the essential Godhead. The Socinians granted Christ's virgin birth and resurrection, without admitting his preexistence or divine nature. The Trinitarians held that Father, Son, and Holy Ghost compose the Godhead, all three being one God as to substance, but three persons as to individuality. The Unitarians, on the other hand, believed that God exists only in one person. The Latitudinarian School of the English Church, the group who favoured freedom of opinion as to church government, worship, or doctrine, was represented by such leaders as Bishops Stillingfleet and Tillotson, Herring and Hoadley. High Calvinism, with its emphasis on divine decrees, had captured the Old Presbyterians, the Independents, and Particular Baptists and in its extreme form, became Antinomianism.[27] Lecky points out:

---

23 Overton, *The Church in England*, 2:202–204.

24 Coomer, *English Dissent*, 63.

25 Overton, *The Church in England*, 2:218ff.

26 Overton, *The Church in England*, 219.

27 Coomer, *English Dissent*, 64–67.

... although a brilliant school of divines maintained the orthodox opinions with extraordinary ability and with a fearless confidence that science and severe reasoning were on their side, yet a latent skepticism and a widespread indifference might be everywhere traced among the educated classes. There was a common opinion that Christianity was untrue but essential to society, and that on this ground alone it should be retained. The indifference with which the writings of Hume and of Middleton were received was as far as possible from arising from a confident faith.[28]

Despite the political involvement, worldly living, and absorption with unresolved controversy which characterized the English Church following the Revolution, it had some strong, spiritual men, among whom were William Law and Henry Venn. "William Law was not only a vigorous opponent of Deism but his *Serious Call to a Devout and Holy Life* of 1728 profoundly influenced John Wesley, and remains one of the monuments of English hortatory literature."[29] Henry Venn of Huddersfield in Yorkshire, was well known as the author of a popular work, *The Complete Duty of Man*, and was credited with being largely responsible for evangelism outside of London. He tried to meet the needs of the people so well that Wesley and Whitefield were not needed in his town.[30]

Despite these efforts of a few evangelical men, the English Church of the eighteenth century stands condemned. It had a great opportunity to raise the spiritual tone of the time, but because of its multiple weaknesses, it failed to meet the challenge.

THE METHODISTS

Against the dark background prevailing generally throughout England, the great spiritual fact of the time, rising within the Established Church, but escaping its bounds in spite of itself, is the Wesleyan Revival—the second Reformation in England. The experience of genuine conversion which came upon John Wesley at the humble meeting in Aldersgate Street "forms an epoch in English history. The conviction which then

---

28 Lecky, *History of England*, 3:9.

29 Williston Walker, *A History of the Christian Church* (New York: Charles Scribner's Sons, 1919), 508.

30 J.H. Overton and Fredric Relton, *The English Church from the Accession of George I to the End of the Eighteenth Century (1714–1800)* (London: Macmillan and Co. Ltd., 1906), 179.

flashed upon one of the most powerful and most active intellects in England is the true source of English Methodism." The societies which sprang up under the leadership of John and Charles Wesley and George Whitefield sought to be a church within a church: more pious, more disciplined, and more evangelistic than the religious body as a whole.[31]

The Methodists, whose establishment of chapels and field-preaching gradually forced their separation from the Church of England, were of two groups. Wesleys' followers were usually considered the genuine Methodists and held to the Arminian interpretation of universal redemption, while George Whitefield, leader of the other group, followed the Calvinistic belief in election.

The Calvinistic Methodists were reinforced "from a quarter least expected, from the seat of wealth and grandeur, in the person of the Countess of Huntingdon."[32] At first her support was largely through the employment of Anglican ministers with evangelistic zeal as chaplains of her household. As a result, she was able to have the truth preached to many of the nobility whom she had invited to her home. Many who entertained strong prejudices against the Dissenters and against the unattractive plainness of their worship, and who equally disliked Wesley's connection on account of his ecclesiastical tactics, classes, bands, and the government of a supreme patriarch, were charmed with the churchly appearance of "Lady Huntingdon's chapels, the crimson seats, the outspread eagles which formed the pulpits and reading-desks, the loud and solemn-sounding organ, the much-loved surplice, and responses in the liturgy."[33]

The societies, the discipline, the peculiar dress of the members are all characteristic features of early Methodism. Despite any criticism that might be aimed at their rudeness of manner, the emotional frenzies they had inspired, or the hierarchical government administered by Wesley, they had their outstanding excellencies. As "diligent indefatigable itinerants," journeying often on foot, they penetrated villages and remote corners of England that had scarcely any previous acquaintance with religion. Their staunch stand against vice of every kind and their zeal for the purest morals brought them persecution and praise alike.[34]

---

31 Lecky, *History of England*, 3:48–49.
32 David Bogue and James Bennett, *History of Dissenters from the Revolution in 1688, to the Year 1808* (London, 1808), 3:94.
33 Bogue and Bennett, *History of Dissenters*, 3:95–97.
34 Bogue and Bennett, *History of Dissenters*, 3:57.

It would be difficult to overstate either the intensity or the far-reaching effects of this movement. It began in 1738 and "manifested itself in a permanent modification of English character, and by consequence in an extensive reconstruction of moral ideals, of religious institutions, of social customs."[35]

THE DISSENTERS

The other religious groups of the day collectively were known as Dissenters, the body of believers who dissented from the Established Church, composed of Presbyterians, Congregationalists or Independents, and Baptists, General and Particular. A review of their status as late as 1793 shows that "they were excluded from all civil and ecclesiastical employment of honour and profit in the kingdom." No Dissenter could hold command in the army or navy in time of invasion; they were barred from the bench and from receiving any kind of university degree; a Quaker could not testify in any criminal prosecution whatever, even as witness to the murder of his father or wife, without denying his religion. A Dissenter who subscribed to the doctrine of the Trinity was permitted to worship, but one who denied it was liable to confiscation of goods and imprisonment. Dissenters paid all taxes and tithes and were made to fill those church offices involving labour and expense, such as churchwarden. They were heavily penalized if they did not serve or provide their own acceptable substitute.[36]

The disabling Acts of the Restoration Settlement had not been revoked, but they were becoming obsolete or were superseded by the Toleration Act. By subscribing to thirty-five of the *Thirty-Nine Articles*, Dissenting ministers were given considerably more freedom, and the congregations were protected against civil disturbance affecting their buildings and worship.[37] The possibility of the Stuarts' return after William and the political turn of events under Queen Anne, however, coupled with the people's resentment of the tyranny of Cromwell's generals, kept the Dissenters in a state of apprehension until the beginning of the Hanoverian succession. "The Dissenters for many years

---

35   Henry C. Vedder, *The Story of the Churches: The Baptists* (New York: The Baker and Taylor Co., 1903), 108.

36   John Rippon, *The Baptist Annual Register* (London: 1790–1802), 1:524.

37   Coomer, *English Dissent*, 95–96.

looked back to that August day as the real birthday of toleration," and received George I as their certain saviour from persecution. Reinforced by the solid support of Protestant Dissenters, the Hanoverians continued to exert their influence on the side of toleration, political though their motives may have been.[38]

A number of wealthy merchants, capitalists, and even some prominent municipal leaders were numbered among the Dissenters, probably by means of the annual Acts of Indemnity. Over the years, their ranks were distinguished by such intellectuals as Baxter, Howe, Calamy, Bunyan, Henry, and Defoe. Seafaring men and tradesmen of the towns subscribed most readily,[39] and by a quiet acceptance of their legal handicaps, they were able to achieve a workable relationship with the government and the Episcopacy. "Speaking generally, Churchmen and Dissenter were content to go their several ways, for in two things they were agreed—enmity to Rome and hatred of 'enthusiasm.'"[40]

In a realm where vigour and zeal might be expected, we find that for the Dissenting bodies, as well as for the Established Church, "it was an era of weakness, declension and demoralization ... it was an age of feeble mediocrity, of rampant unbelief, of gross immorality, where strength and faith and purity might reasonably have been looked for."[41]

Once the Dissenters had great zeal, but, with the Act of Toleration, came the same spiritual paralysis that affected the Establishment. All their strength seemed to have been used in acquiring liberty. "Religion lost all value when it no longer demanded the sacrifice of worldly goods, of bodily health, and life itself."[42]

The same intellectual controversies that disturbed the Established Church also shook the Dissenting churches to their very foundations, and they, too, were enveloped in the "Age of Reason."[43] It is interesting to note the distribution of theological variations among Dissenting bodies in London about 1730:

> The Presbyterians...nineteen Calvinists, thirteen Arminians, and twelve Baxterians. All the Independents...were Calvinists, twenty-seven

---

38 Coomer, *English Dissent*, 5–7.
39 Lecky, *History of England*, 1:252.
40 Coomer, *English Dissent*, 103.
41 Vedder, *Story of the Churches*, 107.
42 Maximin Piette, *John Wesley in the Evolution of Protestantism* (London: Sheed and Ward, 1938), 177.
43 Coomer, *English Dissent*, 107.

thoroughly, and one somewhat dubious; three inclined to Antinomianism, and two, who were disorderly, did not deserve any particular remark. Of the two Seventh-Day Baptist ministers, one was a Calvinist and the other an Arminian. Of the sixteen Particular Baptists, seven were Calvinists, and nine inclined to the Antinomian strain. Five of the eight General Baptists were Arminians, and three Socinians.[44]

Though the eighteenth-century Dissenters come under much the same condemnation as the Church of the Establishment—in an age of materialism, a period of dim ideals, of expiring hopes—the evidences of spiritual life in England existed. Of the influence of Dissenters in promoting true religion, Bogue and Bennett affirm:

> From the restoration to the rise of Methodism, Dissenters stood up alone in defence of the best causes. They alone maintained the depravity of human nature, which no baptismal waters could wash away; they preached the doctrines of justification by faith alone, and regeneration by the Holy Spirit…and they singly dared to protest against the fashionable vices of the nation, at the hazard of being treated as outlaws from society and traitors to the state…The apostasy [sic] of the nation from the sentiments and spirit of the Gospel had been total, but for the Dissenters; by their means a vital spark was preserved, and the nation is now warmed with the spreading flames.[45]

At the outset, the Dissenters were almost united in their hostility toward the Methodist Revival. They feared its Arminianism, which so often led to Arianism,[46] and in the case of the General Baptists, who were Arminian themselves, the support of infant baptism continued to be a stumbling block.[47] They resented the acceptance of lay preachers, the Methodists' exemption from the Toleration Act, and John Wesley's autocracy. For his part, Wesley expressed his own dislike for Dissent and had a way of referring to the Baptists as Anabaptists, a term still bearing the stigma of the Munster excesses. George Whitefield, the Calvinist, was on much better terms with the Dissenters, however, and Philip Doddridge was one outstanding Dissenter with a charitable attitude toward the new movement, even exchanging pulpits with their

---

44 Bogue and Bennett, *History of Dissenters*, 3:378.
45 Bogue and Bennett, *History of Dissenters*, 4:497.
46 Coomer, *English Dissent*, 109.
47 Underwood, *English Baptists*, 149.

preachers on occasion.[48]

A number of minor fanatical sects arose following the religious turmoil of the Commonwealth period but, with the exception of the Quakers, who remain in universal respect and substantial numbers, they have long since disappeared. Their colourful names included Diggers and Seekers, Ranters, and Muggletonians, and over fifty are listed as existing in the seventeenth century. The opening half of the eighteenth century, a time of apathy, however, saw the formation of no new sects.[49]

A word needs to be said regarding the Dissenting distinctives in worship that were keystones in their development. The effectiveness of the hymns of Charles Wesley on the Methodist Revival indicates the extent to which the hymns of Isaac Watts and Philip Doddridge, both Independents, strengthened the arms of the Dissenters. The hymns truly qualified as "the poor man's poetry and the poor man's theology." A definite prejudice against the Prayer Book occasioned the second great characteristic of their worship, extemporary prayer.[50]

THE PRESBYTERIANS

From the time of Queen Elizabeth, the Presbyterian formation within the Church of England sought to rid the Church of the last traces of Romanism and to attain the state of reformation of the Reformed churches of the Continent. For almost 100 years the Presbyterians struggled with the Episcopacy and in 1643 achieved apparent triumph in the Long Parliament, during which the prelacy was abolished and steps were taken to organize the country along the lines of the present Church of Scotland, with Parliament itself taking the place of the General Assembly. Cromwell, an Independent, did not fall in with these aims, so the Presbyterians turned from him and played their part in restoring the monarchy. Their final hopes for building some of their principles into a more comprehensive national church were defeated when the Toleration Act forced them, in 1689, to join the ranks of Protestant Dissenters.[51]

---

48 Coomer, *English Dissent*, 110, 116–117.
49 Coomer, *English Dissent*, 27.
50 Coomer, *English Dissent*, 39.
51 Coomer, *English Dissent*, 10.

A loose association of independent churches replaced the hoped for network of national organization and the term "Presbyterian" became a misnomer. There was no church meeting, not even a membership roll—admission being to a congregation rather than to a church and a statement of belief proving sufficient, regardless of whether the candidate could claim a vital religious experience or not. The looseness of such a system, the failure to check trust-deeds, and the laxity in administering oaths to ministers, bred heterodox doctrine, and Arianism soon caused congregations to split as their only means of protest. The desertion of the popular element of his church usually did not greatly affect the minister because the old Presbyterian meeting houses most often were endowed.[52]

Early in the eighteenth century, the Presbyterians ranked first among the Dissenters,[53] but by the end of the century, Arianism and its attendant Socianism had caused orthodox Presbyterianism to dwindle almost to extinction. The name, "Presbyterianism," came to mean Arianism, Socianism, and Unitarianism, until the formation of the Presbyterian Church of England in 1876 restored it to orthodoxy.[54]

At the outset, some few Presbyterians had joined the Independents, and from 1690 to 1692, these two groups attempted a "Happy Union." The alliance soon broke down over the Antinomian Controversy, however, with only the provincial associations surviving in strength for any length of time.[55]

THE INDEPENDENTS

Small groups of Puritans toward the end of the Elizabethan era began to recognize the hopelessness of finding the reformation they sought within the confines of the Church of England. As Separatists, they went out to become a sect, maintaining that "the Church should consist of men and women who had consciously dedicated themselves to Christ and His service." Their leaders, Robert Browne, Henry Barrow, John Greenwood, and John Henry, were the founders of modern Congregationalism.[56]

---

52 Coomer, *English Dissent*, 11–13.
53 Coomer, *English Dissent*, 10.
54 Underwood, *English Baptists*, 117, 167.
55 Coomer, *English Dissent*, 58.
56 Underwood, *English Baptists*, 32.

Following these beginnings, the expulsion of the Puritan clergy from the Church of England, by the Act of Uniformity in 1662, greatly strengthened the rise of Congregationalism in English life and thought. Henry Jacobs founded the "Mother Church of the Independents" in London in 1616, upon the advice and with the approval of a number of the most eminent Puritan clergy, his own spirit reflecting that of his party in its reluctance to separate and its continued hope for Episcopal reform. Within a few years, the church became Baptist, developing from open to strict membership.[57]

Although superficially the Independent worship services were very similar to those of the Presbyterians, there was a significant difference arising from the fact that the Independents were a "gathered church," a group of believers called together by their personal religious experiences. The Church Covenant was the statement of the body of doctrine to which they subscribed, enabling them to stand strong against the forces of Deism and Arianism[58] and rank first among the denominations as the exponent of true religion.[59]

The hymns of Watts and Doddridge, finding their first general use among the Independents, further gave that movement the solid strength and orthodoxy forfeited by the Presbyterians.[60] Watts felt no call to adapt to "modernism," but, in his doctrinal soundness, went far in preserving the Puritan spirit. Although Doddridge's output was smaller than Watts', the enduring quality was the same.[61]

THE BAPTISTS

Two groups, of separate origin and an important doctrinal difference, composed the English body of Baptist believers. The Particular Baptists earned their name by their Calvinistic belief in the particular redemption of Christ, efficacious only for the elect, while the General Baptists, a much smaller group, held to general or universal redemption.[62]

The Particular Baptists belonged to the English Calvinist Separatists

---

57   J.H. Shakespeare, *Baptist and Congregational Pioneers* (London: The Kingsgate Press, 1906), 172–3, 178.

58   Coomer, *English Dissent*, 16, 19.

59   Bogue and Bennett, *History of Dissenters*, 3:400–401.

60   Coomer, *English Dissent*, 19.

61   Coomer, *English Dissent*, 41–42.

62   Coomer, *English Dissent*, 22.

who grew to accept believer's baptism as the New Testament teaching. They were the "last stage in the evolution of English Separatism as it moved forward to its logical outcome in believer's baptism," arising between 1633 and 1638 from the Henry Jacob church of the Independents and retaining its Calvinistic theology.[63] The General Baptists grew from a somewhat different origin. John Smyth became the founder of the first English Baptist church, when he led a group of exiles in Amsterdam to break away from Brownism on the issue of believer's baptism.[64] He baptized Thomas Helwys, who in turn founded the first Baptist church on English soil, in Spitalfields in 1612.[65] This group, with its roots in Holland, derived its Arminianism from the Synod of Dort which met in 1619.[66] The two groups remained quite separate until their Union in 1892, although they were in complete accord on the teachings of the deity of Christ; baptism of believers by immersion; congregational church government; independence of the local church, yet association for promotion of spiritual life and work; and responsibility of the individual member for the "holiness, vigour, and general efficiency" of his church and associated churches.[67]

English Baptists suffered, wrongly, from the association of their name with the Anabaptists who had led the tragic "Revolt of the Common Man" on the Continent.

> That there was an indebtedness no one can deny, but they were marked off from each other by differences of origin, doctrine, social and political ideals. One point of likeness, the rejection of infant baptism, has blotted out, for many historical writers, the whole field of difference.[68]

At the opening of the eighteenth century, the Baptists had almost disappeared from national life because of the legal restrictions against Dissenters.[69] Theologically, the Particular Baptists were suffering from a deadening Hyper-Calvinism, which led into Antinomianism,[70]

---

63 Underwood, *English Baptists*, 56–57.
64 Shakespeare, *Pioneers*, 125.
65 Underwood, *English Baptists*, 47.
66 Coomer, *English Dissent*, 19.
67 John Clifford, *The English Baptists, Who They Are, and What They Have Done* (London: E. Marlborough & Co., 1881), Appendix of Notes, xviii.
68 Shakespeare, *Pioneers*, 15–17.
69 W.T. Whitley, *A History of British Baptists* (London: Kingsgate Press, 1932), 163.
70 Underwood, *English Baptists*, 128.

while the General Baptists had largely followed the Presbyterians into Arianism, with only a small group remaining to form the orthodox "New Connection of General Baptists" under the leadership of Daniel Taylor in 1769. Other variations existed within the Baptist body. The "Strict" churches offered communion and membership only to those baptized after declaration of belief; "Open Communion" churches were composed of Paedobaptists admitted to communion but not membership; and "Open Membership" churches admitted Paedobaptists to both. A further small grouping included the Seventh-Day Baptists who still worshipped on Saturday.[71]

London Baptists responded in only a limited way to England's Revival during the time of Wesley and Whitefield, producing no evangelist, but we shall see that the awakening was only delayed, to come in force a few years later. The London Baptist Association did take on a new lease of life, but the majority of the pastors were untouched by Methodist zeal, enclosing themselves in Hyper-Calvinism or scholarly studies that failed to touch the current of living. "The way in which the L.B.A. did respond to the new movement was most conservative; it built upon old precedent, it ignored the world at large."[72]

Though many blemishes appeared among the Baptist ministers, evangelical doctrine was still preached in purity by the majority and even with great ability by some. The increase of the number of their congregations is an evidence of their zeal. They did, like the early Methodists, reach the poorer classes in a way the Independents and Presbyterians were not able to do. "It is rather a tempting theory to consider the Presbyterians as the cold intellect of the Dissenting movement and the Independents as the rather clamorous voice; if so, we must treat of the Baptists as its untutored heart."[73]

---

71 Coomer, *English Dissent*, 25–26.
72 W.T. Whitley, *The Baptists of London 1612–1928* (London: Kingsgate Press, 1928), 51–53.
73 Coomer, *English Dissent*, 20.

John Owen

The Puritan divine who was Booth's favourite theologian and
who had a significant influence on his theological development

2

ABRAHAM BOOTH'S
EARLY LIFE

CHILDHOOD, EDUCATION, AND PREPARATION

Abraham Booth, the oldest child in a large farm family, was born at Blackwell, in Derbyshire, on May 20, 1734. In the first year of his life, his parents moved from Blackwell to Annesley Woodhouse, a hamlet in the parish of Annesley, Nottinghamshire, where they occupied a farm belonging to the Duke of Portland. Young Abraham began early to help his father in the support of the family, and while it cannot be established that poverty was their lot, the position of the tenant farmer in this period indicates their limited means. At the age of sixteen, Abraham left the farm and set himself to learning the business of a stocking maker. He was never articled as an apprentice to the trade but managed to support himself until he was twenty-four.[1]

Formal education was not readily available to inhabitants of villages and retired districts in the early eighteenth century. This fact, coupled with limited means may account for Booth's meagre schooling. His friends often heard him say that he had never spent six months in school until he "quitted the farming business." The elder Booth taught his son to read, making it a general practice "to hear him read his lesson every day after dinner."[2] His lack of classroom attendance, however, did

---

1   "Memoir of the Author" in *The Works of Abraham Booth, With Some Account of His Life and Writings* (London: J. Haddon, 1813), 1:xviii–xix. Henceforth, citations from this three-volume edition of Booth's works will be cited simply as *Works* with the appropriate volume number and pagination.

2   "Memoir of the Author" (*Works*, 1:xviii).

not limit the development of his mind, for almost entirely on his own initiative and industry, he learned to write and mastered arithmetic. "And as he grew up... he cheerfully sacrificed the hours usually allotted to repose and recreation, for the pleasure he found in prosecuting [his studies]. When the other members of the family retired to rest, Abraham withdrew to cultivate his mind."[3]

It appears that his principle reason for leaving the farm, with its daylight-to-dark schedule, was his hope of finding more time for his studies. He utilized the additional freedom so well that at the end of almost eight years of diligent study, supporting himself at the stocking frame, he had earned for himself a sizable body of useful knowledge and evidenced considerable intellectual maturity.[4]

Booth's parents were professedly members of the Church of England, but this early period in his life appears to have been influenced directly by the ministry of the Barton Preachers, a group of men whose inclinations were, at the same time, toward Methodism and Independency.[5]

THE BARTON PREACHERS

This group of ministers, from humble walks of life, but with outstanding gifts, included some remarkable personalities. Joseph Donisthorpe, the blacksmith, Francis Smith, Nathaniel Pickering, John Grimley, Samuel Deacon Sr., John Whyatt, and William Smith were but a few of those whose labours are worthy of note.[6]

Samuel Deacon of Ratby, a convert of the Preachers himself, became the pastor of the little church at Barton-Fabis, Leicestershire, which arose as a result of his labours, and there he remained for fifty-two years. This Barton Church, organized in 1745 as a loosely knit society of several communities, divided in 1760 into five Midland churches: Barton, Melbourne, Loughborough, Kegworth, and Kirkby Woodhouse; Ilkiston and Smalley were organized in 1785. The original congregation registered as Independent, but step by step, accepting immersion and then believer's baptism, they came to the General

---

3   "Memoir of the Author" (*Works*, 1:xix).
4   "Memoir of the Author" (*Works*, 1:xx).
5   A.C. Underwood, *A History of the English Baptists* (London: Kingsgate Press, 1947), 150.
6   "Barton-in-the-Beans", *The Baptist Quarterly*, 11(1942–1943):421.

Baptist persuasion.[7] The daughter churches were the foundation stones upon which the Yorkshireman, Dan Taylor, built the New Connexion of General Baptists.

These fearless Barton Preachers endured a vast amount of persecution, along with their congregations, from both the populace and the Established clergy. Indomitable will and evangelistic zeal, however, drove them forward until they had organized a long list of churches. Their practice of immersion occasioned some of these persecutions, as the following account illustrates:

> In 1749, S. Dixon, preached at Moorgreen; was dragged by a mob and put under water in a nearby pond. Several followers of him held farms and houses under Lord Melbourn; and through the ill-will of a neighbor, who was under-steward to his Lordship, were driven from their possessions, on account of their religion. The clergyman of the parish, being a violent enemy to the Baptists took every opportunity to harass them. He endeavoured to frighten or persuade the less informed to take their children to be sprinkled; and would probably have succeeded in some instances, had not their more intelligent friends interfered. This drew down his vengeance on them: and he threatened to prosecute John Alvery, in the spiritual court, for teaching school without a license; but was deterred by an appeal, through Mr. Booth (Abraham's father) to the Deputies appointed to protect the civil rights of dissenters.[8]

The Magistrates heeded an appeal from the Preachers to check these persecutions, and while personal insults upon them stopped, they continued to encounter "hooting, shouting, and similar expression of ill will." Oblivious to these harmless demonstrations, the ministers continued their work, gaining ground daily.[9]

BOOTH'S CONVERSION

An average boy raised in the traditions of the Church of England might have delighted in joining with the hecklers and persecutors, interrupting the Baptist worship services, but there is no hint that either Abraham or the Booth family participated in the antagonistic attitudes so common

---

7   Underwood, *English Baptists*, 150.
8   Adam Taylor, *The History of the English General Baptists* (London, 1818), 1:252.
9   "History of the New Connection of General Baptists", *The General Baptist Magazine*, 1 (1798):407.

at the time. The Memoir attached to Booth's *Works* simply says:

> The first direction of his mind towards the dissenters took place when he
> was about ten years of age; and was occasioned by the preaching of some
> plain and illiterate teachers belonging to the denomination of General (or
> Arminian) Baptists who occasionally visited his neighborhood. They drew
> the attention of the family; and under their discourses our author was first
> awakened to a concern about the salvation of his soul.[10]

The preaching of these men apparently made a permanent impression
upon him, and his concern deepened. Booth and his parents appear to
have been among the first-fruits of the Barton Preachers' ministry in the
small church at Kirkby-Woodhouse. The youth applied to the society of
General Baptists for admission into their communion, on profession
of faith, in 1755 and was baptized by Mr. Francis Smith, at Barton.[11]
Though then only twenty-two years of age, he joined these despised
people and soon became eminently useful.[12]

BOOTH'S MARRIAGE AND SCHOOL AT SUTTON-ASHFIELD

Two years later, at the age of twenty-four, Booth married Miss Elizabeth
Bowmar, the daughter of a neighbouring farmer, and they lived together
happily for more than forty years. This important step, with the increase
in responsibility, seemed to have occasioned his leaving the weaving
industry and setting up a school at Sutton-Ashfield, where the young
couple worked in partnership.

> Mrs. Booth assisted in the undertaking by instructing the female pupils
> in the useful branches of needle work, for which she had been eminently
> qualified by her education, in respect of which she had been privileged far
> beyond what commonly falls to the lot of young women in the same rank
> of life. They also wished to take a few boarders, but that part of the plan
> met with but little success, for the number seldom exceeded two or three.[13]

Nothing more is known of the school venture except that Booth is

---

10 "Memoir of the Author" (*Works*, 1:xix).
11 "Memoir of the Author" (*Works*, 1:xix).
12 Taylor, *History*, 2:26.
13 "Memoir of the Author" (*Works*, 1:xx).

referred to by subsequent writers as having operated a school, and that in the year 1758, "His own work was largely at Sutton, where he was a schoolmaster."[14]

WITH THE GENERAL BAPTISTS

By the time of his marriage, Abraham Booth had achieved, almost entirely by his own efforts, a very credible education for his day. His evident thirst for knowledge might well have made him long for university training, but Dissenters were denied entrance into English universities, and the General Baptists had no institutions of higher learning of their own at this time.

They had no universities, colleges, or academies to supply them with ministers, but they believed it to be the duty of Christians earnestly to desire spiritual gifts, but especially that they might prophesy; and that every church ought to be a nursery, to nurse up and cherish among themselves; to embrace any among them, whether learned or unlearned, that were likely to be useful in the Lord's work.[15]

ITINERANT PREACHING

As a member of a small group, with only a limited number of preachers and leaders, Booth doubtless had frequent opportunities to lead prayer meetings and even the weekly worship services. It is quite evident that the members of his religious community recognized his qualities for spiritual leadership. "They accordingly invited him to assist occasionally in the public preaching of the Word; and so rapid was his improvement that, in a little time he was considered as a leading person among them."[16]

As the General Baptists grew in numbers throughout the district, Booth aided them increasingly. He was frequently at Melbourne, Barton, Loughborough, Disworth, and other places, at a distance of twenty, thirty, and even forty miles from home, "preaching the glad tidings of salvation to his fellow sinners, according to the views which

---

14   "Sutton in Ashfield", *The Baptist Quarterly*, 4(1928–1929):372.
15   Taylor, *History*, 1:430–431.
16   "Memoir of the Author" (*Works*, 1:xx).

he then had of divine truth."[17]

The society, managed by a group of elders and ministers, was by this time beginning to develop some peculiar features borrowed from the Moravians, in their practice of graduating their members into four classes, the highest numbering 160. Such an organization proved unwieldy and caused considerable difficulty to many of its members.[18]

William Kendrick, who had been operating a school at Barton, was perhaps the best trained leader the Barton Society had but, around 1759, he was excluded from the group for immorality. The group then turned for leadership to Abraham Booth and J. Grimley, two of their other preachers who possessed some advantages over their associates and had for some time studied the nature of a church of Christ, its organization, and the proper discipline.[19] It was Booth who suggested the New Testament plan of organizing local churches, for the group obviously needed and desired to form the large society into local congregations.[20] Mr. Kendrick's exclusion gave them their opportunity to propose the formation of distinct churches, on the grounds that resident pastors would assist greatly in extending the cause. It was agreed, after much discussion, to divide into five distinct and independent societies.

This division, discussed earlier, became effective in 1760, and when they had completed arrangements for fraternal intercourse, they found that they had about twenty stations with ten pastors and other officers.[21] These men were carefully distributed among the churches, with regard for the feelings of individuals and for the good of the whole. The ministers held monthly meetings for mutual assistance and quarterly conferences, in rotation, where one or two sermons were preached. Many of the members from a distance attended and expressed much satisfaction and edification.[22]

GENERAL BAPTIST SUPERINTENDENT AT KIRKBY-WOODHOUSE

Booth was selected to superintend the Kirkby-Woodhouse congregation, though he was not an ordained minister at the time.

---

17 "Memoir of the Author" (*Works*, 1:xxi).
18 W.T. Whitley, *History of British Baptists* (London: Kingsgate Press, 1932), 218.
19 Taylor, *History*, 2:44.
20 Whitley, *History*, 218.
21 Whitley, *History*, 218.
22 Taylor, *History*, 2:46.

During the four or five years he served the church, "for reasons which do not appear, he declined to take upon himself the pastoral office."[23]

Despite his lay status, he was evidently considered the pastor. A list of the "Five Midland Churches" shows "Kirkby-Woodhouse, Abraham Booth, Minister."[24] This son of a Nottinghamshire farmer, "a convert of the Midland Evangelical Revival,"[25] was now in a position to devote more time and energy to preaching, which he was said to do "with considerable acceptance and success."[26] The congregation at Kirkby-Woodhouse, drawn from the small community and the Booth family, seems to have followed him with devotion.

Booth's interests were not limited to his own congregation as indicated by records of activity in two other churches. Melbourne was the second of the churches formed at the Barton division in 1760, and consisted of about forty members. Francis Smith and Thomas Perkins were ordained joint pastors. In the ordination, Abraham Booth gave the charge from Acts 20:28, "Take heed therefore unto yourselves, and to all the flock, &c."[27] Mr. Booth and the other ministers assisted in the preaching at the Gamston church where the pastor, Mr. Jeffrey, was failing from age.[28]

HIS FIRST PUBLICATION

As a General Baptist, Booth held the Arminian doctrine of universal redemption and was a strenuous advocate for the universality of divine grace. In his enthusiasm for this doctrine, he wrote and printed a poem entitled, *On Absolute Predestination*, published first in pamphlet form[29] and then in a collection of hymns, by W. Kendrick of Barton.[30] No copy of this work has been discovered in the course of this research, but the writer of the Memoir attached to the *Works* says it is a poem,

---

23 "Memoir of the Author" (*Works*, 1:xxi).
24 J.H. Wood, *A Condensed History of the General Baptists of the New Connexion* (London: Simpkin, Marshall and Company, 1847), 169.
25 Underwood, *English Baptists*, 179.
26 "Memoir of the Author" (*Works*, 1:xxi).
27 "Memoir of the Author" (*Works*, 1:xxi).
28 Taylor, *History*, 2:257–258
29 "Memoir of the Author" (*Works*, 1:xxi).
30 W.T. Whitley, *A Baptist Bibliography* (London: Kingsgate Press, 1916), 1:178.

...in which the fervour of his zeal for what he then esteemed truth, had vented itself in reviling the doctrines of election and particular redemption, in language as replete with contumely and reproach as is to be found in the writings of Wesley or Fletcher.

The circulation of this pamphlet, that he later denounced, was not wide and "must have been a source of painful reflection to him in the subsequent period of his life, when his mind was better instructed on this sublime subject."[31] In his preface to the "last corrected edition" of *The Reign of Grace*, Booth records his own judgement:

> To this edition of *The Reign of Grace*, I have made large additions. The principal of which is, an entire chapter upon "Election"; which renders the scheme of doctrines more complete, and the contents of the book more answerable to the title. I also thought it my duty, in a particular manner, to bear a public testimony to that important part of revealed truth; having in my younger years greatly opposed it in a poem *On Absolute Predestination*. Which poem, if considered in a critical light, is despicable; if in a theological view, detestable; as it is an impotent attack on the honour of divine grace, in regard to its glorious freeness; and a bold opposition to the sovereignty of God. So I now consider it, and as such I here renounce it.[32]

THE CHANGE OF SENTIMENTS: THE PARTICULAR BAPTISTS

The thought of Abraham Booth appears to have been shaped, up to this stage in his life, through self-education and the efforts of the earnest but untutored Barton Preachers with their limited understanding of the Bible. Ernest F. Kevan, referring to Booth's poem, *On Absolute Predestination*, concludes that, "As is usually the case with such violent opponents of this doctrine [Sovereign Grace], he possessed only a distorted view of the whole subject through an insufficient study of the Scriptures."[33]

There is no direct clue in Booth's writings as to how he came to understand differently, beyond his statement of the enlightenment that accompanies earnest Bible study and prayer. In his work, *The Death of*

---

31   "Memoir of the Author" (*Works*, 1:xxi).

32   Booth, *Works*, 1:4.

33   Ernest F. Kevan, *London's Oldest Baptist Church (Wapping 1633–Walthamstow 1933)* (London: Kingsgate Press, 1933), 118.

Legal Hope, he refers to his previous understanding of the doctrine of sovereign grace:

> Through the ignorance of his mind, the pride of his heart, and the prejudice of his education, he [Abraham Booth], in his younger years, often opposed it with much warmth, though with no small degree of weakness; but after an impartial inquiry, and many prayers, he found reason to alter his judgment; he found it to be the doctrine of the Bible, and a dictate of the unerring spirit. Thus patronised, he received the once obnoxious sentiment, under a full conviction of its being divine truth. Now he considers the eternal, discriminating love of God, in the choice of his people, as the original source of all that glory they hereafter expect. To the distinguishing love of the Father; to the redeeming blood of the Son; to the almighty agency and sanctifying operations of the Divine Spirit, he now desires to ascribe the whole unrivalled honour, of a complete, eternal salvation.[34]

An exact date is not given for Booth's change of conviction, but it appears to have taken place in 1762 or 1763. Dr. W.T. Whitley makes the following statement relative to this change:

> One of its [the General Baptists] rising men was Abraham Booth, who had been scandalized at the hyper-Calvinism of the Particular Baptists, and had written against it. But the teachings of Fuller proved to meet his needs and supply a body of doctrine acceptable and necessary. He quitted his early friends at the age of thirty...[35]

It will be seen that the reference to Andrew Fuller's influence on Booth's theological views at this time is impossible, for the simple reason that Fuller was only ten years of age at the time Booth changed in his sentiments.

Booth realized that this change of doctrine was such as to make it utterly impossible for him to continue among the General Baptists, and he had too much integrity to try to conceal the difference. Meetings were held to investigate the doctrinal differences, and each party produced its best arguments on behalf of its respective tenets. Since neither party could convince the other, they mutually agreed to part.[36]

In his farewell sermon to the Kirkby-Woodhouse Church, Booth

---

34 Booth, *Works,* 1:377.
35 Whitley, *History,* 232.
36 "Memoir of the Author" (*Works,* 1:xxiv).

preached from the parable of the unjust steward, pointing out that fraud and concealment may win the friendship of men, but alliances so gained are peculiarly inexcusable. Scripture, reason, and conscience join in endorsing "universal fidelity to accountable creatures, and especially to the ministers and professors of religion, in the view of the great day of account, when they must all give up their stewardship."[37]

Booth's separation from the General Baptists around the year of 1765 caused a temporary suspension of his preaching activities. Within a short time, however, a place called Bore's Hall was procured and licensed at Sutton-Ashfield, where he gathered a small society of Calvinists or Particular Baptist adherents and resumed preaching.[38]

In addition to his own pulpit and his weekday work, Booth began itinerant preaching in Nottingham, Chesterfield, and throughout the region. His exertions during this period were astonishing:

> He had to labour throughout the week, for the support of a family every year increasing, and even then become numerous. He had frequently to travel the distance of twelve or fifteen miles on the Lord's day morning and afterwards to preach twice or thrice, during the day, for which the only remuneration he accepted was barely the expense of horse hire, which at no time exceeded ten pounds a year... [39]

BOOTH WRITES *THE REIGN OF GRACE*

The doctrinal point on which Booth had split with the General Baptists, that of particular redemption or election, was naturally the subject of his most intensive study during these beginnings with the Particular Baptists. A series of sermons preached first at Sutton-Ashfield and afterwards at Nottingham and Chesterfield, contained the form and most of the substance of his greatest work, entitled, *The Reign of Grace*.

When the manuscript was finished, Booth showed it to some friends, probably with no view to immediate publication. He was yet an obscure individual, even within the circle of his own denomination. One of these friends was favourably impressed and reported to Henry Venn of Huddersfield in Yorkshire concerning the excellency of the

---

37 "Memoir of the Author" (*Works*, 1:xxiv).
38 "Memoir of the Author" (*Works*, 1:xxiv).
39 "Memoir of the Author" (*Works*, 1:xxiv).

work. Venn, one of the few evangelically-minded clergymen of the Church of England, requested the manuscript, and it was sent to him. He further urged Booth to publish *The Reign of Grace* and, with a view to making it more generally known, wrote a recommendatory preface which accompanied the first and second editions. The work was first published in April 1768 and soon attracted general attention.[40]

As soon as it was sent to press, Venn wrote Lady Huntingdon, recommending to her this work that had so impressed him:

> I have just been the means of publishing a work which, all things considered, your Ladyship will doubtless think a very extraordinary one. The author is very poor, has seven children, and was never taught more than to read or write. The title of the book is, *The Reign of Grace, from its Rise to its Consummation.* Some things there are in it which I am sure would exceedingly delight you; and from the rage with which they rail against me at Halifax, for causing it to be published, I trust the old serpent feels it strike at his throne.[41]

He praised the work for its "marks of genius joined with feelings of a Christian heart; in his reasoning, clearness and force, and in his doctrine an apostolic purity." He predicted, too, that this publication would earn Booth a better situation, one "proper for a man whom God hath endowed with abilities, and a taste for good Learning," so that he would no longer be dependent upon his own manual labour.[42]

Venn, sometime afterwards, moved to Huntingdonshire and Booth to London, but they continued to correspond, and when Venn visited London, he almost always made a friendly call upon his non-conformist friend. Likewise, when Booth had occasion to visit that part of the country, "he failed not to show his respect for him by taking up his abode at the parsonage house."[43]

On one of these visits, Venn expressed a desire to hear the author of *The Reign of Grace* preach but could think of no way to do so since he dared not present him in his own pulpit. However, he had a pulpit constructed for him in his own kitchen, assembled a congregation, and "the consistent and determined opposer of all religious establishments,

---

40 "Memoir of the Author" (*Works*, 1:xxvi–xxvii).

41 Aaron Crossley Hobart Seymour, *The Life and Times of Selina Countess of Huntingdon* (London: William Edward Painter, 1841–44), 2:24.

42 Seymour, *Life and Times of Selina Countess of Huntingdon*, 2:24.

43 "Memoir of the Author" (*Works*, 1: xxvi).

was engaged in holding forth the word of life, under the roof of a dignified clergyman of the national church."[44]

As soon as Booth's publication was in circulation, the Countess of Huntingdon distributed a number of copies in every direction, recommending the author to several of her dissenting friends of the Baptist denomination in London. She sent several copies to Dr. Andrew Gifford, the assistant curator of the British Museum, London, requesting him to use his utmost efforts in promoting the welfare of the deserving author.[45]

Some of the members of the church in Little Prescott Street, Goodman's Fields, London, then without a pastor, read the book and being impressed with it, brought his name before the church. A committee of three members was appointed to visit and hear him preach. The Church Minutes record their sentiments and the subsequent events:

> [Booth] was a sound nervous Gospel Minister.... They invited him to spend a Lord's Day or two with the people with whom they stood connected. The Revd. Mr. Booth came to Town Saturday the 18th June, and the next Day according to appointment preach'd for us, as he did also the two succeeding Lord's Days to the general satisfaction of the Church, insomuch that it was thought proper after sermon in the afternoon of the Lord's Day July 3rd to stop the Church to know their mind concerning him.
>
> And the Question being put whether this Church should give him an invitation to return to us again as soon as his affairs would permit. It was unanimously carried in the Affirmative, not one hand being held up for the Contrary Opinion.

Before Booth's return in August, it is recorded they:

> ...agreed that a Solemn Day of Prayer should be observed by this Church the next week, to implore the Divine Blessing on the steps which had been taken towards the settling of a Pastor over us—and that the Lord would vouchsafe us his presence in our publick assemblies in the meantime—The same was accordingly observed, and it was remark'd by several that a spirit of prayer evidently appeared on that occasion.[46]

---

44 "Memoir of the Author" (*Works*, 1:xxvi–xxvii).

45 Seymour, *Life and Times of Selina Countess of Huntingdon*, 2:25.

46 Church Minutes, Little Prescott Street Baptist Church, 3:121.

Abraham Booth returned to London and preached four more consecutive Sundays. The church voted unanimously to call him to the pastorate in the business season, September 18, 1768, and a copy of a most affectionate letter, signed by thirty-four male members is incorporated into the Minutes. Abraham Booth accepted the call, and his original letter, dated October 1, 1768, is now one of the church's treasures.[47]

From lowly beginnings, Abraham Booth, by tremendous effort and concentration, without the benefit of any formal education, without family position or influence, had now risen to a first class opportunity. The estimate of Dr. W.T. Whitley is implied in his reference to this move to London: "He quitted his early friends at the age of thirty, and expounding his new beliefs in *The Reign of Grace*, was promptly called to take charge of the premier Particular Baptist Church in the world, at [Little] Prescott Street."[48]

---

47 Kevan, *London's Oldest Baptist Church*, 90–91.
48 Whitley, *History*, 232.

William Fox

One of Booth's deacons and one of his strongest supporters,
who played a key role in the development of the Sunday School

3

THE PASTORATE OF THE LITTLE PRESCOTT STREET BAPTIST CHURCH

Abraham Booth left his Midland home and friends, the Sutton-Ashfield Baptist Church, which he had pastored from its beginning in about 1765 and moved his family into the metropolis of London. His call to the Little Prescott Street Baptist Church was perhaps the greatest promotion to which a minister of his denomination could then aspire. It was the oldest, strongest, and most influential Particular Baptist church in the world at the time.

The church's beginnings were so early and unusual, they merit attention. A congregation of Protestant Dissenters of the Independent persuasion assembled in London in 1616 and formed the Henry Jacob Church mentioned in Chapter 1. Several members of the society were dissatisfied because the group had relaxed their principles of separation and were receiving infant baptism from the English Church. Those who did not agree were allowed to leave and form a new congregation after their own convictions. They were constituted a distinct church on September 12, 1633. Almost all received a new baptism because they considered their infant baptism invalid. The records are confused as to whether John Spilsbury was the pastor of this first church, although by 1638, when William Kiffin, Thomas Wilson, and others of the same persuasion, were dismissed to the new church upon their request, it was established that Spilsbury was their leader and that the group rejected infant baptism on any grounds.

In the present state of evidence, we may say with certainty that in 1638, there was either the first Calvinistic Baptist Church with John Spilsbury as its pastor, containing Samuel Eaton, Mark Lucar, and others, or that in the same year, there were two Calvinistic Baptist Churches in London, the one under John Spilsbury and the other under Samuel Eaton.[1]

The Little Prescott Street Church developed from the Spilsbury Church.[2]

Other records from anonymous manuscripts, attested by the official records of the Star Chamber and High Commission, indicate that many of the first members of this church were prisoners in the Clink and Gatehouse Prisons at the very time of the organization of the church. These Independent bodies were illegal at this time and were hounded, persecuted, and imprisoned. The charter group met just outside the actual boundary of London in Wapping, a section chiefly inhabited by seafaring men. They had no building of their own, most likely holding their Sunday services in a warehouse on Old Gravel Lane.[3]

The earliest Church Minute Book discovered opens in 1676. Prior to 1689, it was perilous for a Baptist church to keep records, for until the Revolution in 1688, Baptists had no legal existence. During their first fifty years, the Baptists were continually under the necessity of issuing Confessions of Faith, in order to clear themselves of the slander and libel that were poured upon them. Records from the time of Cromwell and the Protectorate indicate that there were men of position and influence in the membership. Pastors Spilsbury, John Norcott, and Hercules Collins led the ever-increasing society until, in 1686, the Minutes records a membership of 387 men and women. The church built its first meeting house in 1687, in James Street, Wapping, completing it in time to observe the ordinance of the Lord's Supper on August 7 of that year, the first service in the new building. The deeds setting out the lease of the land are the very earliest such documents in England and today are among the rich historical treasures of the present

---

1   J.H. Shakespeare, *Baptist and Congregational Pioneers* (London: The Kingsgate Press, 1906), 180–183.

2   Ernest F. Kevan, *London's Oldest Baptist Church (Wapping 1633–Walthamstow 1933)* (London: Kingsgate Press, 1933), 15–16.

3   Kevan, *London's Oldest Baptist Church*, 24–27. The author examined the Little Prescott Street Church Minutes personally, but the theft of his notes, before mentioned, necessitated dependence upon Mr. Kevan for almost all of the quotations from these records.

Church Hill Baptist Church, Walthamstow.[4]

Following Hercules Collins, three men of average talent served successively as pastors: Edward Elliot, William Curtis, and Clendon Dawkes. In 1726, however, Samuel Wilson came to lead the church in a period of growth and prosperity. Under his ministry, they built a new meeting house in Little Prescott Street, Goodman's Fields, one of London's finest residential sections during the eighteenth century. Samuel Burford came in 1755 and served until April 16, 1768. A few months later, Abraham Booth accepted the call as pastor,[5] and the church, which had grown from persecuted beginnings, long before the laws of the land permitted it an existence, to a position of strength and influence, entered upon an outstanding epoch of service.

THE ORDINATION AT LITTLE PRESCOTT STREET

The Minute Book of the Little Prescott Street Baptist Church gives this account of the ordination service of their new pastor:

> Mr. A. Booth was solemnly set apart to the pastoral office over us February 16, 1769. At which Solemnity the following Ministers were principally concerned; viz., Mr. Clarke, who opened the Business of the Day, put the Questions to the Church, & required the minister's *Confession of Faith*; Mr. Thompson, Dr. Stennett & Mr. Clarke assisted in laying-on of Hands, Mr. Thompson praying on that occasion; Mr. Wallin gave the charge, & Dr. Stennett preached to the Church: besides Mr. Jenkins, Mr. Reynolds and Mr. Macgowan, who all assisted in Prayer.[6]

Undoubtedly it was a source of encouragement to Booth, then thirty-four years of age, that the Countess of Huntingdon, "being at that time in London, was present on the interesting occasion, and ever after maintained a friendly intercourse with Mr. Booth."[7]

The order of the service indicates that the church was asked to give an account of the steps taken in calling Abraham Booth. After this, they were asked to ratify this call by voting again by a show of hands.

---

4 Minute Book of Little Prescott Street Church, Vol. 1, and Deed parchment in possession of successor church, The Church Hill Baptist, Walthamstow, London.

5 Kevan, *London's Oldest Baptist Church*, 48–49.

6 Minute Book, Little Prescott Street Church, 3:123–124.

7 Aaron Crossley Hobart Seymour, *The Life and Times of Selina Countess of Huntingdon* (London: William Edward Painter, 1841–44), 2:25.

Booth was asked to recount the steps he had taken relative to their call, following which he delivered his Confession of Faith, and a summary of his now Calvinistic doctrine, to be considered more fully in Chapter 5.[8] The introductory discourse, delivered by William Nash Clarke, A.M., was published along with the charge, sermon, and *Confession of Faith*. It was long thought that this publication had vanished, but Seymour J. Price reports discovering a copy in 1939.[9]

PREPARATIONS FOR AN EFFECTIVE MINISTRY

Booth was doubtless fully impressed with the greatness of his new opportunity and responsibility. His need for further preparation was clear to him and served to stimulate his vigorous mind. He set about meeting this need immediately by mastering Latin and Greek, with the aid of an eminent classical scholar, a former Roman Catholic priest. No record disclosed to date gives this gentleman's name, but Booth always highly praised his erudition.[10]

In his efforts to increase his proficiency in languages, Booth never lost sight of his primary aim to make all learning serve his preaching and pastoral work. He never sought to become an accomplished Hebrew scholar. Greek was his first concern because it was basic to his understanding of the New Testament; and proficiency in Latin opened the inexhaustible stores of theological works from the Continent, by such men as Witsius, Turretine, Stapferus, Vitringa, and Venema. Few men of his time were better informed on the Popish controversy.

> Ecclesiastical history was a favourite subject with him; and the writers of that class, viz. Dupin, Cave, Bingham, Venema, Spanheim, and the Magdeburg Centuriators, were familiar to him; as were also Lewis, Jennings, Reland, Spencer, Ikenius, Carpzovius, Fabricius of Hamburgh, and others on the article of Jewish Antiquities. Among the writers of his own country, there was none that engaged so much of his regard as Dr. John Owen.... from whom there will be found more quotations in his writings than from any other author... except... the sacred volume.[11]

---

8   "Memoir of the Author" (*Works*, 1:xxviii).
9   Seymour J. Price, "Abraham Booth's Ordination, 1769", *The Baptist Quarterly*, 9 (1938–1939):242–246.
10   "Memoir of the Author" (*Works*, 1:xxxvii–xxxviii).
11   "Memoir of the Author" (*Works*, 1:xxxviii–xxxix).

Booth, aiming at the highest learning consistent with his pastoral responsibility, devoted long hours to study, without failing in the unending duties which the church presented. The pulpit of the Little Prescott Street Baptist Church placed him in a position of prominence in denominational work for which his "extensive range of interests, his mighty intellect, his keen insight and his broad outlook fitted him." He never aspired to titles, and an American university feared to offer him the degree of Doctor of Divinity, lest he should decline it.[12] British editions of his works bear no evidence of his A.M. degree conferred by Brown University in 1774.[13]

There had been a sad mortality among the Baptist preachers in London between 1765 and 1772, occasioned by the deaths of Brine, Anderson, Flower, Burford, Straton, Gill, and Messer. Dr. W.T. Whitley comments on it as a form of blessing, however. "In one way, we may be thankful, for half of these had emptied their churches with reactionary preaching; and it is with the arrival of Abraham Booth in London that the Baptist churches began to revive."[14] A similar statement is made by A.C. Underwood who speaks of the small effect of the Evangelical Revival on the Baptists of London, "but here too, the necessary new leaders appeared. John Rippon, Abraham Booth, and Joseph Ivimey were the men who did the most to change the situation, and all three came from the Provinces."[15]

The findings of Robert G. Torbet, an American Baptist historian coincide with the above.[16]

THE SUCCESS AND INFLUENCE OF BOOTH'S MINISTRY

The Minute Book of the Little Prescott Street Church shows that under the ministry of Booth there were numerous baptisms and a constant increase in membership. If these were the only indications of a faithful and successful ministry, there would be ample reason for gratitude.

His sermons, born of hours of study, meditation, and prayer, were the work of a mature Christian mind and spirit, and those that

---

12   Kevan, *London's Oldest Baptist Church*, 120.

13   *Historical Catalogue of Brown University, Providence, R. I., 1764–1894* (Providence, R. I.: Press of P. S. Remington & Co., 1895), 331.

14   "Bunhill Fields: The Place and the Records", *The Baptist Quarterly*, 5 (1930–1931):225.

15   A.C. Underwood, *A History of the English Baptists* (London: Kingsgate Press, 1947), 178.

16   Robert G. Torbet, *A History of the Baptists* (Philadelphia: The Judson Press, 1950), 101.

were published reveal closeness of reasoning and a doctrinal unity throughout. Booth was not given to a great amount of controversial preaching, but, when the occasion seemed to demand it, he did not hesitate to attack error with righteous indignation. His uncompromising stand for the "genuine gospel," as he saw it, is attested in his statement from *The Reign of Grace* regarding the "charitable" attitude of those who allow for a wide range of interpretation in basic Christian doctrine:

> ... though such conduct may be applauded, under a false notion of Christian candour, and of a catholic spirit; though it may be the way to maintain a friendly intercourse among multitudes whose leading sentiments are widely different; yet it will be deemed, by the God of truth, as deserving no better name, than a joint opposition to the spirit and design of his gospel. For such a timid and lukewarm profession of truth is little better than a denial of it—than open hostility against it. To seek for peace at the expense of truth, will be found in the end, no other than a wicked conspiracy against both God and man.[17]

A year after he came to London, Booth published *The Death of Legal Hope*, which he dedicated to the Little Prescott Street Church in a statement that reveals his pastoral hopes and concerns for them. It reads in part:

> That you may have a growing acquaintance with divine truth in all its branches, and an increasing affection one to another *for the truth's sake*: that the life, and fervour, and amiable simplicity of primitive Christianity, may be conspicuous in your worship and conduct; that faith may abound in your hearts, and the fruits of righteousness adorn your conversation; is the sincere desire and earnest prayer of your affectionate friend, and willing servant, in the gospel of our common Lord, A. Booth.[18]

He considered his congregation as a trust from God for which he would be required to give a full account. His own statement relative to his sense of responsibility to the church reveals this:

> I have never left my people since I first settled with them, more than two Lord's days at a time. Had I left them so much as some pastors have

---

17 Abraham Booth, *The Reign of Grace, From its Rise to its Consummation* (Philadelphia: Joseph Whetham, 1838), xi.

18 Booth, *Works*, 1:332–333.

left theirs, I have no doubt my people would have left me as theirs have left them.[19]

He worked so diligently as shepherd of his flock, that he was known frequently to travel the streets, the whole length of London, in search of a member who had been absent from the services.[20] He was unwearied in his ministries to the poor, the rich, the saint, and the sinner. One time a woman in his congregation left him a sizeable legacy, which he quietly deposited in the Bank of England to the account of some of her poor relations whom he had discovered.[21]

One of Booth's significant services to his denomination was his part in a number of ordinations of young ministers, including William Newman, first principal of Stepney Academy, T. Hopkins, Joseph Swain, Thomas Hunt, Joseph Dermer, William Jarman, and Benjamin Coxhead. Most of these men became eminent servants in the Baptist churches in and around London. In these ordinations, as in all services, Booth was particularly sensitive to the needs and condition of his hearers. The ordination of Joseph Dermer had run overly long when it came Booth's time to address the people. Instead of delivering his prepared message, he observed, "where weariness began devotion generally ended," and because of the length of the service, he limited himself to reading his text and making a few brief extemporaneous remarks on what already had been said.[22]

The periodical literature of the late eighteenth century reports the Little Prescott Street pastor's frequent participation in funerals in and around London. His wide interest and deep sympathy seem to have made him a favourite for this service of consolation. The numerous funeral discourses and addresses at the grave which were published, reveal that they were no great eulogies of the character of the deceased, nor departures of oratory, but genuine statements of the Christian evaluations of life and death. They "may be held up as models of address which young ministers would do well to copy after, when called to officiate on those mournful occasions."[23]

In 1775, the pastor led his congregation in forming the "Prayer

19 Joseph Ivimey, *A History of the English Baptist* (London: Isaac Taylor Hinton, 1830), 4:368.
20 Ivimey, *History*, 4:lxxii.
21 John Westby-Gibson, "Booth, Abraham", *Dictionary of National Biography*, 5:373–374.
22 "Ordinations" in John Rippon, *The Baptist Annual Register*, 2 (1794–1797):348–349.
23 "Memoir of the Author" (*Works*, 1:lix).

and Alms Society," an organization to care for the needy in the church membership and the surrounding neighbourhood, as far as available funds would permit.[24] "Observations" on this Society, from 1841, reported that the visitors prayed with the persons they were visiting and advised them spiritually according to their needs. It operated only in instances of sickness and poverty and was credited with being "the means of bringing many sinners to the knowledge of Christ, and of comforting many poor and afflicted saints." A "Sister Beckingham" bequeathed £300 to this society for relieving the poor of the church, and through the years the fund was often extended to many demands outside the congregation. Typical beneficiaries were: Pastor Samuel Mee of Maze Pond; a poor friend of the Gosnall Street Church; and the distressed Spitalfields Weavers in 1793.[25]

Under Booth the church accepted other opportunities for service as they arose. When the "Meeting House" of the Millyard Church, under the pastoral leadership of Mr. Thomas, was burned in 1790, Little Prescott Street lent its church premises free of charge for nine months. Frequent special prayer meetings were held by the congregation "on account of the deep distress of the labouring poor, through the extreme dearness of provisions," for a church without a pastor, or for some other kind of crisis.[26]

The church initiated an extraordinary procedure in 1779 because of "the great number of cases of insolvency in business among the Church members." These cases were carefully investigated by the church, with a committee of two making inquiries and examining books and accounts.[27]

The Church Minutes indicate the purchase of a book for the registration of the births of children to the members of the church. This book is now in Somerset House.[28] All of the activities, insignificant though some of them may appear, indicate that Abraham Booth was alert to a wide range of opportunity for Christian service.

The Sunday School of the Little Prescott Street Church, organized in 1798, was one of the first in London. Twenty-three years earlier, in 1775, Booth had addressed the church in a business session on behalf

---

24 Kevan, *London's Oldest Baptist Church*, 95.
25 Kevan, *London's Oldest Baptist Church*, 95.
26 Kevan, *London's Oldest Baptist Church*, 95–96.
27 Kevan, *London's Oldest Baptist Church*, 96.
28 Kevan, *London's Oldest Baptist Church*, 96.

of just such an organization, observing:

> That, for five or six month past, he had had the public Catechising of Children much upon his mind, & desired to know the sense of the Church as to the propriety & utility of it. Which being considered, it was unanimously agreed, to be proper & adapted for usefulness to the rising generation among us. And it was agreed, that the Church be stopped the fifth Lord's Day in the next month, that our brethren & sisters may be more generally informed of this resolution, & to conclude on a suitable time for beginning & carrying on the exercise.[29]

No clue is given for the delay of twenty-three years in establishing the Sunday School, unless it was the referral of the resolution to consideration at a regular service of the church. Booth had not been there long, and perhaps his new idea was not readily accepted; the probability is that enough members opposed it to postpone action upon the recommendation indefinitely. It will be noted that Booth's first attempt to establish a Sunday School preceded by six years Robert Raikes' organization at Gloucester of the first recognized Sunday School in this great movement.

The Church Minutes refer no more to the Sunday School. Fortunately, however, the first Minute Book of the Sunday School, now in possession of the Walthamstow Church, gives an account of its beginnings:

> August 27th, 1798. The underwritten by unanimous consent formed themselves into a committee for the purpose of transacting the business relative to an intended institution of a Sunday School in the vicinity of Goodman's fields: Names as follow viz.
>
> Mr. Squire in the Chair. Messrs. Wilkinson, Bull, Johnson, Fairey, Wyatt, Palmer, Chambers, Capes.[30]

The new committee considered Rules and Order for regulating the school, which the pastor revised and submitted for their approval on September 10, 1798. Reference is made to the twelve rules or articles adopted, but the secretary failed to record them. Two amendments read:

---

29 Quoted Kevan, *London's Oldest Baptist Church*, 97.
30 Quoted Kevan, *London's Oldest Baptist Church*, 97–98.

Mr. Fairey moved the following amendment to the 2d Article viz. "that the children attend at Mr. Booth's Meeting only." Resolved.

Resolved that this Institution be denominated the Goodman's Fields Sunday School and that it open (Providence permitting) the first Sabbath in October next.[31]

Originally the school was managed by a committee appointed from the subscribers supporting it; later the teachers constituted the committee. In October 1798, this group decided to purchase 100 spelling books, Watts' *Songs*, Watts' *Catechism*, candles, slates, pasteboards, inkstands, pens, and articles of clothing for poor and ill-clad children. A room was hired near the church, and the hours of the school were from two until four o'clock Sunday afternoons.[32]

Within a few months, the pupils of the school made such rapid progress that a public service was held for them to read and repeat their catechism before the benefactors. An order, recorded in the Minutes, for the printing of 10,000 tickets for the school indicates a progressive spirit in the body. Teachers were volunteers and were accepted only after a period of probation. There seems to have been no lack of volunteers. Six teachers taught each Sunday, and the girls' and boys' work was kept separate. In October 1799, it was further decided "That Twelve of the most forward boys be instructed in Writing for one hour every Monday evening." This later led to the employment of a schoolmaster, and on October 13, 1801, Mr. Pendrid was appointed "Master of the Boys' School on his own conditions and … the allowance annexed … 2s 6d. per day."[33]

A new development in March 1801, was the summer day school, opening at eight and closing at four-thirty daily. It must be remembered that there were few free schools in England in those days, hence the magnitude of the church's work appears the greater. A further progressive move was made later in 1801, when an evening school was begun, meeting each Sunday from six until eight p.m., for the exclusive purpose of religious instruction. Thomas Coles, A.M., of Aberdeen, Booth's assistant pastor, directed this work.[34]

Booth preached a special sermon on behalf of his Sunday School in

---

31 Quoted Kevan, *London's Oldest Baptist Church*, 98.
32 Kevan, *London's Oldest Baptist Church*, 99.
33 Quoted Kevan, *London's Oldest Baptist Church*, 100.
34 Kevan, *London's Oldest Baptist Church*, 100.

August 1801. In 1803, when the Sunday School Union was founded, the Goodman's Fields School joined immediately, and its records show that it participated in all the great children's rallies in the succeeding years. William Hiett, one of the first scholars, later became superintendent, occupying the position for fifteen years. Statistics show that in the first thirty-five years of its work, the school admitted over 4,500 children.[35] Thus it can be seen that this one organization had "been the means of leading hundreds to Christ, either in childhood, or, by the abiding effects of the teaching, in the later years of life."[36]

BOOTH'S LEADERSHIP OUTSIDE HIS OWN CONGREGATION

The Society of London Ministers of the Particular Baptist Persuasion, better known as the Baptist Board, was founded in 1724.[37] This group was concerned with the needs and problems of most of the Baptist churches in London and its vicinity.

In the spring of 1771, when Booth had been at Little Prescott Street Church for about two years, he was invited onto the Board.[38] For the next thirty-five years, he appears as perhaps the leading member of this group. Scarcely an important matter is recorded in the Board Minutes without Booth's name as president, secretary, chairman, or member of committee.

In this connection, Booth participated in the deliberations and decisions of the Managers of the Particular Baptist Fund, an organization formed in 1717 whose "chief designs in this affair are the honour of God, the keeping up of his public worship in several parts of this kingdom, the edification of the churches, and the relief of many poor labourers in the Lord's vineyard."[39] This organization will be discussed in Chapter 4.

Problems of discipline of ministers occasionally came to the Board. In connection with their exclusion of Thomas Oliver, pastor at Hammersmith, in May 1793, Booth was asked to frame the notification:

---

35 Quoted Kevan, *London's Oldest Baptist Church*, 101, from the Sunday School Minutes.

36 Kevan, *London's Oldest Baptist Church*, 102.

37 Seymour J. Price, *A Popular Baptist History of the Baptist Building Fund* (London: Kingsgate Press, 1927), 15.

38 "The Baptist Board Minutes", *Transactions of the Baptist Historical Society*, 6 (1918):82. Henceforth, this item will be cited as "Baptist Board Minutes" with the appropriate pagination.

39 W.T. Whitley, *A History of British Baptists* (London: Kingsgate Press, 1932), 203.

Sir, I here return the Testimonials given you by the Church under the care of Mr. Garniss. Am glad to find you acknowledge your disorderly conduct toward that church in leaving it as you did; and that the members of it bear such a testimony in your favour. I laid your papers, on Tuesday last, before the Brethren at the Coffee house; and after some conversation respecting those papers, the ministers present unanimously agreed in requesting me to inform you, That your company at the Coffee house is not desirable to them. I most sincerely pray for your happiness, & remain, Sir, Your cordial well-wisher.

A. Booth.[40]

John Martin also was excluded from the Board, for his seditious statement in a sermon that if the French should invade England, many Dissenters, both Baptists and Paedobaptists, would join them. The Board called upon Booth to participate in the investigation of the matter.[41]

The issue between Martin and the Board continued through the Minutes for some five years. Two of Booth's members, James Smith and his son-in-law, Joseph Gutteridge, appeared along with others seeking to persuade the Board to reinstate Martin. They agreed that if Martin made "such concession as we think should be satisfactory to Booth whom we consider he has grossly insulted both in conversation & in print," they would not object to Christian intercourse with him.[42]

Booth's response, in the form of a letter to the Board, revealed his generous spirit:

... My own mind is made up on the disagreeable subject, yet ... I am utterly averse from the thought of his being kept out ... because I think he is undeserving ... I therefore deprecate its being hereafter said, "Mr. Martin would have been long ago restored to his connection with the General Body had it not been for the prejudice, the pride, and the obstinacy of A. Booth."[43]

Churches with internal disputes, discord between churches, and matters of doctrine were considered by this group. The Minutes

---

40 "Baptist Board Minutes", 89.
41 "Baptist Board Minutes", 92
42 "Baptist Board Minutes", 97, 124.
43 "Baptist Board Minutes", 98.

indicate, in addition, their concern for occasional matters outside denominational limits, such as a hearty support of vaccine inoculation, and a pledge to spread of information regarding it.[44]

In the Minutes of the March 26, 1799 meeting, evidence is given of the Board's regard for their long-time member, Abraham Booth:

> The Brethren from their great respect to their worthy President Mr. Booth and sympathizing with him under his present indisposition, Resolved unanimously, to afford him, in rotation, any assistance in their power, which he may find convenient. Resolved that our Secretary transmits a copy of this resolution to Mr. Taylor, one of the Deacons of Mr. Booth's church.[45]

Two lecture series, outside the Baptist denomination, the Lord's Day Morning lectures, and the Lord's Day Evening Lectures, sought Booth's assistance, and his name appeared repeatedly in the schedules of ministers through the years at the turn of the century.[46]

The Particular Baptist Monthly Meetings in London, a regular activity for about the last twenty-five years of Booth's life, indicate that he was eminently active in promoting the denominational fellowship during that period. John Rippon records the lists of these services with all ministers and their participation in each service. The ten Particular Baptist churches in London and Southwark, constituting the Particular Baptist Fund, led in rotation at these meetings. Booth seldom missed his turn, and he and his church were among the most faithful supporters of the Fund.[47]

Thus, the scope of Booth's service was far wider than his ministry to the Little Prescott Street Church. As his activities multiplied and his health began to fail, two assistant pastors, first Thomas Coles, then William Gray, were engaged to aid him in his later years. The congregation in its letter to Gray's church in Wiltshire, recognized their pastor's faithful service, both to his own congregation and the denomination:

> ... For a long course of years he [Mr. Booth] has maintained an honourable and laborious station in the Church of God. His attention of late years has

---

44 "Baptist Board Minutes", 99.
45 "Baptist Board Minutes", 95.
46 See John Rippon, *Baptist Annual Register*, 3 (1798–1801), *passim*.
47 See John Rippon, *Baptist Annual Register*, 1–4 (1790–1802), *passim*.

not been confined to his Pastoral duties, but, in a sense, it may truly be said, "The care of all the churches has been, and still is, upon him."[48]

CANDIDATES FOR THE MINISTRY

Evidence of the church's spiritual vigour can be seen in the number of its members who entered full time Christian service. A careful study of the Little Prescott Street Church Minutes for the period of Booth's ministry, indicates that the following members began preaching before that congregation: Gill, Crawford, Hornblow, Edward Greene, Thomas Hunt, Mackenzie, Thomas Sheraton, Joseph Harris, Chamberlain, and George Capes. In addition to these, Booth's two assistants, Thomas Coles and William Gray, doubtless received valuable training and inspiration in their associations with Booth.

A few of the group became well-known throughout England and possibly beyond. Thomas Sheraton (1751–1806) was the furniture designer, who, in addition to publishing works on his craft, did a few devotional studies as well. In 1798 he brought to the church a scheme for evangelizing the villages around London and led in carrying on the work, with a good measure of success. This work is not described in the Minutes, but evidently was some form of open-air preaching and teaching. In 1800, Sheraton accepted the pastorate of the church at Darlington.[49]

Thomas Hunt, ordained in 1793, left an account of the church's procedure in encouraging its young men in the ministry. Fortnightly the church held a conference on religious subjects, at which time the young men interested were given opportunity to try their preaching ability before the congregation. When one of then had preached, Booth summarized the leading idea, then gave his opinion upon the subject. Hunt said that after a few of these practice sermons, he was invited to preach in one of the regular church services. After six months of such application, the church accorded the young man an appropriate acknowledgment of his progress:

> ...a time of solemn prayer was set apart for divine direction, and suitable portions of Scripture were read by our pastor. At the following meeting

---

48   Quoted Kevan, *London's Oldest Baptist Church*, 105.
49   Kevan, *London's Oldest Baptist Church*, 102.

held May 18, 1791, the church unanimously agreed to give me a call to the work of the ministry, which I cordially accepted in the fear of God, looking up to him for assistance.[50]

Following one of the regular services some time later, Booth addressed Hunt on the attitudes and problems of a minister. The next Sunday, said Hunt, "I entered upon the public ministry, and delivered a discourse, being my first sermon, from Psalm xxvii.14."[51] The Minute Books indicate this was standard procedure with one after another of these young men.

Thomas Coles came to assist Booth in 1801, having just finished his work at Aberdeen and having been awarded the A.M. degree (Master of Arts).[52] He served as temporary assistant for some six weeks before the church formally invited him to become their assistant pastor. After a short time, the Church reluctantly released him that he might succeed the late Benjamin Beddome at Bourton on the Water.[53] The Bourton congregation, in writing to the Goodman's Fields Church that they were desirous of having Thomas Coles as pastor, entreated the church to allow him freely to consider their invitation. The Little Prescott Street Church acceded to this request "with a degree of Christian resignation, which does them great honour."[54]

On August 4, 1813, Coles preached a sermon at Broadmead Church, Bristol, before the Bristol Education Society, which was published and described by a reviewer as a "plain, solid, and judicious discourse."[55] It was very similar to Booth's *Pastoral Cautions*, indicating a degree of the pastor's influence over his assistant.

To replace Coles, the church extended a call to William Gray of the Wiltshire Church. He accepted the invitation and, in his own words from the Minute Book, was "sensibly affected with the prospect of standing by the side of such a person as your venerable pastor."[56] Arriving in London in 1802, he remained with the church until Booth's death in 1806. In October of that year, he was ordained pastor over the Plymouth Dock Baptist Church, where he served until 1809. He then

50 "Ordinations" in John Rippon, *Baptist Annual Register*, 2 (1794–1797):119–120.
51 "Ordinations" in Rippon, *Baptist Annual Register*, 2:120.
52 *The Evangelical Magazine*, 10 (1802):147.
53 Kevan, *London's Oldest Baptist Church*, 105.
54 *The Evangelical Magazine*, 10 (1802):147.
55 "Account of Religious Publications", *The Baptist Magazine*, 6 (1814):168.
56 Quoted Kevan, *London's Oldest Baptist Church*, 105, from the Sunday School Minutes.

entered upon a most fruitful ministry at Chipping Norton, utilizing his house as an academy for the training of young men. During his pastorate, the church served several village stations, and religion flourished in the town and surrounding villages. Long lists of baptisms are given, and there was recorded concern over the purity of the fellowship, with discipline being exercised rigorously. The evangelistic and educational emphasis, carried over into his own pastorate from his Little Prescott Street training, confirm that Gray had the great advantage of being the assistant of Abraham Booth. Gray resigned in 1825 to become pastor of the College Street Church, Northampton.[57]

These young men were fortunate to have a pastor with the spirit and mind of Abraham Booth. A correspondent of *The Baptist Magazine*, after visiting Booth not long before his death, wrote down some of his conversation for publication. Two sections of advice to young ministers, a brief résumé of his *Pastoral Cautions*, are peculiarly fitting here:

Advice respecting the Pulpit
Never study a sermon with the design of displaying your abilities; but always aim to promote the glory of God.

Endeavour to improve your understanding by reading the Scriptures and praying for divine assistance.

Never forget while you are preaching to others that you are a sinner yourself.

Take care and not attend to publick [sic] work as the mere duty of office.

Pray not as a minister, but as a poor sinner. If you wish to be comfortable in your work, pray for much of the life of religion in your own soul.

Advice respecting Conduct
Be not frequent in your visits to any lady living alone; I have seen much mischief resulting from such conduct.

Never visit any of your hearers who are rich, without a particular invitation; give them no cause to think you want either their food or their money.

Be home with your wife and family early in the evening; many a minister's wife has been rendered miserable through the inattention of her husband.

Have nothing to do with making matches among your people; let the men find their own wives, and the women their own husbands; this is no

---

57   F. H. Rollinson, "Chipping Norton Baptist Church, 1694–1944", *The Baptist Quarterly*, 11 (1942–1945):284.

part of your business, Sir.

Be cautious how you make a will for any of your people; and never be an executor or guardian for any.

Advise not the rich to lend to the poor, nor lend any thing yourself, unless you are first satisfied that you can afford to lose it all.

Be not surety for any one.[58]

THE DAUGHTER CHURCHES OF LITTLE PRESCOTT STREET

The new calico-printing industry in Lancashire attracted many workmen from London, where several of them had been members of Little Prescott Street Church. In 1782, a group of those workmen founded a Baptist church at Preston, receiving the full approval of the home church and the blessing of Abraham Booth. Benjamin Davis became their pastor.[59]

In 1796, Sarah Mears was dismissed from the Little Prescott Street Church to become one of the first members of the Baptist church at Connellsville, Pennsylvania.[60]

Mare Street Church, Hackney, was organized in 1798, with Booth's assistance, from four members from the Little Prescott Street Church and four other Baptists. Thomas Burford, Elizabeth Burford, John Holman, and Deborah Marsom, after considerable conference with Booth and the deacons, were dismissed to unite with others, in forming themselves "into a distinct church, of the same faith and order with ourselves."[61]

The Hackney Church Minute Book gives a full account of its organization on May 13, 1798, with Abraham Booth conducting the service. He addressed the church on the solemnity of this situation and read a long statement of faith, signed by the eight people who made up the new church. He further addressed them on the Scripture, "In whom ye also are builded together for an habitation of God through the Spirit" (Ephesians 2:22).[62] John Rance was ordained as pastor on October 3, 1798, and remained there, successful, honoured, and beloved until his

58 "Mr. Booth's Conversational Advice and Remarks", *The Baptist Magazine*, 2 (1810):18.

59 "James Bury", *The Baptist Quarterly*, 5 (1930–1931):384.

60 Kevan, *London's Oldest Baptist Church*, 103.

61 Quoted Kevan, *London's Oldest Baptist Church*, 103 from Church Minutes.

62 Quoted Kevan, *London's Oldest Baptist Church*, 104 from Church Minutes.

death in 1807.[63]

SOME OUTSTANDING DEACONS UNDER BOOTH'S MINISTRY

In the thirty-seven years Abraham Booth was pastor at Little Prescott Street, the church produced a number of outstanding Christians. Some of the greatest of these were the deacons serving the church, who also became useful in service of the denomination. Personal association, perhaps the strongest character-forming power in existence, seemed to provide mutual blessing and inspiration for Booth and his deacons.

William Taylor, a hosier, come to London in 1750, at about twenty years of age. He was one of the last people baptized by Rev. Samuel Wilson, pastor at Little Prescott Street until his death, and Taylor served as deacon from 1768, the year before Booth's arrival, until his death in 1811.[64] Taylor, a bachelor and apparently having no relatives dependent upon him, was free to devote his means to the Societies which interested him.[65] He openly contributed to the Particular Baptist fund, of which he was one of the treasurers, and on various occasions, his pastor, Booth, presented fifty pounds from an anonymous friend, which Joseph Ivimey says he had reason to know was Taylor. The founders of the fund were accustomed to say, "We hope Mr. Booth's friend will live for ever."[66] A more complete discussion of Taylor's benevolences will be given in the next chapter.

In his will he requested that if Booth took any notice of his death from the pulpit, he wished that nothing should be said of him by way of character. He appears to have shared the spirit of his pastor and friend who left a similar injunction, "that nothing should be said of him in a funeral sermon, and that no more than twenty pounds should be expended in his funeral."[67]

Taylor had given generously to his church, the Particular Baptist Fund, ministerial education, the relief of aged ministers, and to him goes the honour of purchasing the premises of Stepney Green for Stepney Academy. "This was the stroke that entitles Mr. Taylor to the

---

63 "Baptist Board Minutes", 124.

64 Ivimey, *History*, 4:585, 589.

65 George P. Gould, *The Baptist College at Regent's Park* (London: Kingsgate Press, 1910), 21.

66 Ivimey, *History*, 4:589.

67 Ivimey, *History*, 4:588.

homage and respect of the Baptist denomination."[68]

Transactions of the Baptist Historical Society gives a condensed statement concerning Joseph Gutteridge, another of Booth's deacons:

> Gutteridge, Joseph, 1752–1844, Member of [Little] Prescott Street; Treasurer Particular Baptist Fund; Treasurer of Baptist Education Society, 1804; Deputy chairman of the Dissenting Deputies; Founder of Stepney College, 1809; Mill Hill School, Camberwell Church, and Sunday School Society; Early supporter of Baptist Missionary Society, Treasurer Stepney, 1811–1827.[69]

When his father died, Gutteridge, still a youth, inherited his business. He succeeded so well that soon he was independent and able to devote a vast amount of his time to Christian enterprises. In 1778, the year after their marriage, Mr. and Mrs. Gutteridge were baptized by Booth. He was elected deacon in 1786, but made a statement to the Little Prescott Street Church as to why he should not accept the office. The church, however, "moved and unanimously resolved, That the objections were not, in our view, sufficient to justify his declining the office."[70] He accepted and remained a deacon until his death, over fifty-eight years later, in 1844.

He was one of the founders of the Sunday School Society, one of the earliest supporters of the Baptist Missionary Society, and was largely responsible for moving its central office to London. For about twenty years he was a member of the executive committee and for a while the treasurer of the Society.[71] Gutteridge also served as manager, along with William Fox and William Taylor, of the Society for the Relief of the Necessitous Widows and Children of Protestant Dissenting Ministers.

He rendered outstanding service as Treasurer of the Particular Baptist Fund. The Little Prescott Street Church, aided by Gutteridge, was generous in its support, as the following statement indicates:

> Let it not be forgotten that to the influence of the pastors of this church, especially to that of Mr. Booth, and to one of its deacons, Joseph Gutteridge, Esq. the Baptist Fund is chiefly indebted.[72]

---

68 Kevan, *London's Oldest Baptist Church*, 136.
69 *Transactions of the Baptist Historical Society*, 7:205.
70 Kevan, *London's Oldest Baptist Church*, 137.
71 Kevan, *London's Oldest Baptist Church*, 137.
72 Ivimey, *History*, 4:590.

Joseph Gutteridge also became treasurer of the Baptist Education Society when it was formed in 1804, and though it was not all they had hoped for, Gutteridge and Taylor supported it, prayed, and waited. Soon their hopes materialized in the founding of Stepney Academy in London. Gutteridge was the first treasurer of the Academy, was the one instructed to engage the first tutor, and was a committee member until his death. In 1836, when he sat for a bust for the Managers of the Fund, the Little Prescott Street Church procured a similar bust and ordered it to be placed in the vestry.[73] An observation as to the value of Gutteridge's life to his pastor and church may be quoted here:

> This was the type of man Mr. Booth had to support him. It is true that Mr. Booth shines by the brightness of his own light, but who is to say how much his successful ministry and prosperous church owed to such a deacon?[74]

William Fox is the third great deacon of Booth's church whom we shall consider. He was born in 1736 in Gloucestershire. After coming to London, he built up a large business as a draper in Cheapside.[75] He joined the Little Prescott Street Church; was elected deacon at the same time as Joseph Gutteridge; was the organizer of the Sunday School Society; was the first treasurer of the home missionary society;[76] and a Manager of the Society for the Relief of the Necessitous Widows and Children of Protestant Dissenting Ministers.[77]

At the Jamaica Coffee House in London, a group of Baptists held a meeting in May 1785, and William Fox first publicly proposed his plan for the universal education of the poor in biblical knowledge. The group appointed a committee, offered subscriptions, and planned another meeting to which clergy, ministers, and laymen of other denominations were to be invited. Before the next meeting, Fox learned of the work of Robert Raikes, corresponded with him, and as a result of those letters, the assembly voted for a Sunday project rather than a weekday one as Fox had first proposed. At this large and representative gathering on September 7, 1785, presided over by Jonas Hanway, an organization called "The Sunday School Society" was formed "for the support

---

73 Kevan, *London's Oldest Baptist Church*, 138–139.
74 Kevan, *London's Oldest Baptist Church*, 139.
75 Kevan, *London's Oldest Baptist Church*, 139–140.
76 "An Index to Notable Baptists", *Transactions of the Baptist Historical Society*, 7 (1921):202.
77 "The Widows Fund" in John Rippon, *Baptist Annual Register*, 3 (1798–1801):428.

and encouragement of Sunday Schools in the different counties of England."[78]

Questions have been raised as to the credit due either Fox or Raikes as founder of the Sunday School movement. In its first stages, Raikes gave freely of his counsel and cooperation. He followed Fox and his fellow-workers with interest, and his brother, Thomas Raikes, at one time Governor of the Bank of England, was a member of the Committee.

The Society's records clarify the relative positions of Raikes and Fox as evidenced in a letter which Fox wrote to Raikes in September 1785:

> The fire which you have had the honour to light up in Gloucester having now reached the Metropolis, will, I trust, never be extinguished but with the ignorance of every individual throughout the kingdom.[79]

In June 1787, Raikes was given honorary membership in the Society, on the basis of his being the "original founder as well as a liberal supporter of Sunday Schools." Documents show that Raikes conceived and worked out the idea and thus is to be credited as the founder, while William Fox was the architect of the movement who more than any other person made it national and worldwide.

In a short time, through the vigorous policy of Fox's Society, hundreds of Sunday Schools sprang up. Fox promoted the idea that every church should have a Sunday School as an integral and necessary part of its church life.[80]

The modern Sunday School owes much to this Baptist deacon of Little Prescott Street, who was inspired and supported by his pastor, Abraham Booth. Joseph Ivimey describes Fox as, "the glory of the Baptist Denomination and one of its brightest ornaments."[81]

---

78 Price, *Popular History*, 15.
79 Cited John Carroll Power, *The Rise and Progress of Sunday Schools. A Biography of Robert Raikes and William Fox* (New York: Sheldon & Co./Boston: Gould & Lincoln, 1863), 86.
80 Kevan, *London's Oldest Baptist Church*, 141–142.
81 Kevan, *London's Oldest Baptist Church*, 142.

William Carey

The "father of the modern missionary movement," whom Booth did
much to support in the early years of Carey's ministry in India

4

THE GREAT RELIGIOUS
AND SOCIAL MOVEMENTS
OF HIS TIME

The pastoral ministry of Abraham Booth, primarily in connection with the internal affairs of the Little Prescott Street Baptist Church, makes a comparatively complete picture of a busy and faithful spiritual leader, but the great heart of the man would not permit him to limit his activities to his own congregation. Other causes needed his vision, his intellect, and his spiritual wisdom.

THE PARTICULAR BAPTIST FUND

A few weeks after the Act of Toleration in 1689, a general invitation from the Particular Baptist ministers in and about London, signed by William Kiffin, Hansard Knollys, Benjamin Keach, Richard Adams, and others, was sent to Baptist churches far and wide. More than 100 churches were represented at a meeting in London, from September 3 to 12, 1689.[1] Among other things, they resolved to raise by free will offering a fund to be applied to the following purposes:

> To aid churches unable to maintain their own ministry; to send ministers to preach both in city and country, where the Gospel hath, or hath not been

---

1   George P. Gould, *The Baptist College at Regent's Park* (London: Kingsgate Press, 1910), 1–2.

preached, and to visit the churches; and finally, to assist those members that shall be found in any of the aforesaid churches that are disposed for study, having an inviting gift, and are sound in fundamentals, in attaining to a knowledge and understanding of the languages, Latin, Greek and Hebrew.[2]

This effort collapsed, largely from opposition to the educational policy of the Assembly, and nearly a quarter of a century passed before the London Particular Baptists renewed the attempt to organize. Their aim was the same as before, a fund being a prime objective, but the next effort was limited to congregations in and about London.

Six churches responded to the appeals, and the first meeting of the managers was held on June 6, 1717. Other churches joined the next year, and the Fund increased until, within five years, it had reached between £2,000 and £3,000. A part of this was set aside for the education of ministers, but the Education Society was not organized until 1752. The amount was never great, and even in 1771 the managers had less than £700 at their disposal for all purposes.[3] Toward the end of the century, however, with the strenuous efforts of Booth and some of his deacons, the Fund grew in size and usefulness. In 1805, the now inactive Education Society transferred its capital, £1,300, to the Fund, stipulating that it was to be used to assist in its educational work.[4]

The object, here, is not to give a detailed history of the Fund, but to show the significant part Abraham Booth played in supporting and promoting its work throughout his London ministry.

During the last quarter of the eighteenth century, the Fund organization was made up of ten London churches. The annual reports in Rippon's *Register* also list gifts from outside of London, citing Joseph Kinghorn's church in Norwich particularly and encouraging other churches to follow its example (Kinghorn was educated from the Education Society funds). Collections were made annually in the ten London churches, but the greatest amounts came from wealthy individuals who gave large sums or left property or annuities at death. Eight members of Booth's church are listed as giving a total of £24,050 between 1777 and 1821. These are only the larger bequests. There were many donations of £50, annual gifts by the members of the church who

---

2 Gould, *Baptist College*, 2.
3 Gould, *Baptist College*, 13–14.
4 Gould, *Baptist College*, 16.

wished to be Managers of the Fund.[5]

The support and leadership given to the Particular Baptist Fund by Abraham Booth, through the Little Prescott Street Baptist Church and through his personal influence beyond, cannot be measured. Perhaps he was able to multiply his ministry many times over through this agency.

LONDON BAPTIST EDUCATION SOCIETY FOR ASSISTING STUDENTS

Gould reports that in 1720, a committee was appointed to consider the education phase of the Particular Baptist Fund (1717). It recommended that £300 of South Sea Stock and the income from it be set aside immediately for educational purposes. This amount grew from specific gifts, but was too small to accomplish much.[6]

In London, on August 6, 1752, a meeting of twelve ministers and others founded the London Baptist Education Society for Assisting Students, resolving:

1. Agreed unanimously that it is a desirable thing to make some provision for assisting young men in their education for the ministry.

2. Agreed that the Persons to be encouraged in this Design be members of some Particular Baptist church, and that they be recommended as having promising gifts for the ministry by the Church and that they be approved by the Society.[7]

The plan was apparently for the students to live together in London, and to be instructed by a tutor appointed by the society. They were to be under the direct supervision of the Committee, and £20 per annum was to be paid for each student. The first two students proved disappointing and had to be dismissed. Problems of tutors, of student lodgings, of unsatisfactory students, and such, plagued the ventures throughout the whole forty years of its existence. Different plans were proposed, with the students moving from London and being dispersed among different teachers, but eventually the project lapsed

---

5   Joseph Ivimey, *A History of the English Baptist* (London: Isaac Taylor Hinton, 1830), 4:589–590.

6   Gould, *Baptist College*, 13–14.

7   Gould, *Baptist College*,14.

into a state of inaction and neglect. Dr. Whitley comments on the difficulties encountered with a number of the students, "Indeed, if the besetting temptation of the General Baptists was heterodoxy, that of the Particular Baptist was antinomian immorality."[8] As mentioned, in 1805 William Taylor, the sole surviving trustee, transferred its capital of £1,300 to the Particular Baptist Fund, with the provision that it be employed in its educational work.[9]

London Baptist interest in ministerial education had not abated, however, and a new attempt was backed by Abraham Booth in 1804, who was then in his seventieth year. On August 10, at a meeting held at the King's Head, in the Poultry, a Society was formed to assist in the training of young men for the Christian ministry.[10] Foremost among the promoters, along with Booth, were Joseph Gutteridge and William Taylor, two of his deacons, and William Newman, pastor of Old Ford. Gutteridge accepted the office of treasurer, and Booth prepared the appeal for support which indicates the purpose and scope of the Society.[11]

Booth also drafted the rules of the Society, governing admissions to assistance and all matters pertaining to responsibility of the individual accepting aid. Some of the rules are as follows:

>...no person shall be taken under the patronage of this Society, who is not a Member of a Baptist Church, that avows those doctrinal sentiments which are generally denominated Calvinistic, and is recommended by such a Church...Any person so recommended and approved may be placed under the care of a Minister professing the same sentiments; and a suitable compensation for board and tuition shall be made to such Minister...that no person be continued longer than two years on the Society's Fund.[12]

As in 1752, there were those who desired to found an academy in or around London, but others deemed it "expedient to attempt something upon a more humble, though perhaps not less useful scale, than had been originally projected."[13] Although overruled in their academy plans

---

8   W.T. Whitley, *The Baptists of London 1612–1928* (London: Kingsgate Press, 1928), 55.
9   Gould, *Baptist College*, 14–16.
10   Gould, *Baptist College*, 16.
11   Gould, *Baptist College*, 16–17.
12   Gould, *Baptist College*, 18.
13   Ernest F. Kevan, *London's Oldest Baptist Church (Wapping 1633–Walthamstow 1933).* (London: Kingsgate Press, 1933), 121.

in 1804, Booth, his deacons, and others waited for a more opportune time. Booth died in 1806, but his spirit moved on in the enterprise. Four years after his death, his deacon, William Taylor, made a gift of £3,600 to the Society which purchased property in Stepney and made plans for opening a school.[14]

Commenting on Taylor's gift to the Baptist Education Society, Joseph Gutteridge, Treasurer, declared that when he recalled the influence exerted on Taylor by his pastor Abraham Booth, he was almost ready to say, "Here we behold, in this establishment, the fruit of his [Booth's] labours."[15]

The Baptist Academical Institution, Stepney, opened its doors to receive its first three students on Monday, April 8, 1811, with William Newman as president. Through the efforts principally of Abraham Booth and his deacons, William Taylor and Joseph Gutteridge, the Particular Baptists of central and southern England now had a college serving their region just as Bristol Academy, in operation for a generation, and Yorkshire Academy, recently opened, were ministering in their localities.[16]

BOOTH'S OPPOSITION TO SLAVERY AND THE SLAVE TRADE

When William Wilberforce introduced his motion to abolish the slave trade on February 26, 1793, much work had been done to prepare the nation. All manner of evidence calculated to align Parliament against the inhumane business was assembled: the revolts in French Santo Domingo; the testimony of seamen as found by Thomas Clarkson; and the testimony of slaves themselves.

Petitions from every part of the kingdom were being presented to Parliament for its abolition. Abraham Booth took an active interest in promoting and circulating a petition, expressing his abhorrence and that of the Little Prescott Street Baptist Church, of the slave traffic. He also preached a special sermon on the subject from Exodus 21:16, "*Commerce in the Human Species, and the Enslaving of Innocent Persons, Inimical to the laws of Moses and the Gospel of Christ*," which was

---

14   George Pritchard, *Memoir of the Rev. William Newman, D.D.* (London: Thomas Ward and Company, 1837), 230.

15   Gould, *Baptist College*, 21.

16   Gould, *Baptist College*, 19, 43.

published at the request of the church and widely circulated,[17] going through three English, one Dutch, and one American edition.

David Lawrence, Philadelphia, published the American edition, before the end of 1792, with a special note to American readers, preceding the text:

> The following discourse on a subject, which grosses the attention of the humane, being exceedingly scarce in this country, and very great inquiry made after it, by many who have heard it; it has been suggested, that an American impression of the same, would prove highly acceptable to the man of Benevolence, and the Christian... [18]

Booth and his church also made a generous offering towards the expenses which attended the application to Parliament. The slave trade was not suppressed until eight years afterwards, but there is no doubt that Booth essentially contributed towards its abolition as the following statement indicates:

> ...this is the opinion of the most competent judge of the subject, the celebrated antislavery advocate, Clarkson. In his work entitled "The Abolition of the Slave Trade," &c. that inestimable philanthropist has given a list of names of the principal benefactors, who by their writings, money, and influence, assisted in this enterprise of mercy; and among them, to his immortal honour, is found that of our never-to-be-forgotten, and still-lamented, Abraham Booth.[19]

BOOTH'S SUPPORT OF THE FOREIGN MISSION MOVEMENT

The Baptist Missionary Society, organized in Kettering on October 2, 1792, needed every assistance. It naturally turned for support to the London Baptists, a large body possessing considerable wealth. Abraham Booth has been misrepresented on his early support of the Missionary Movement, due to the overcautious attitude of two of his deacons, which was wrongly put to his account.[20] Some interesting

---

17 Ivimey, *History*, 4:369.

18 Abraham Booth, *Commerce in the Human Species, and the Enslaving of Innocent Persons Inimical to the Laws of Moses and the Gospel of Christ* (London: C. Dilly; T. Knott, 1792), preface to the American Edition.

19 Ivimey, *History*, 4:369.

20 Kevan, *London's Oldest Baptist Church*, 123.

details appear in the report of the first London meeting on behalf of the mission enterprise:

> By the invitation of T. Thomas to whom, amongst others, Fuller had written, twenty three laymen and eight ministers (more than half of the whole) met in Devonshire Square. Abraham Booth was absent, unwell. Stennett urged caution. Booths deacons, Fox and Gutteridge were definitely hostile.[21]

Actually the support in London, in great measure, centred in Booth, and the committee in Northampton looked to him for much London leadership. Dr. Whitley specifically informs us that "Abraham Booth was the only London minister who at first backed the Baptist Missionary Society."[22]

The Society at their November 13 meeting, a month after their organization, faced the problem of finding a suitable person to appoint as their first missionary. The minutes relate their consideration of John Thomas:

> ...the Committee was informed that Mr. John Thomas (a Baptist minister, who for a few years past has been learning the Bengalese language, and preaching to the natives), was then in London, and that he much wished, by subscription, to return to his work, and to take some fellow-labourer with him. The Committee then agreed to make inquiry into Mr. Thomas's character, principles, &c.[23]

Andrew Fuller journeyed to London and inquired concerning Thomas. He talked with Booth, looked over the graphic letters which Thomas had written from India, met Thomas, and invited him to come to Kettering to meet the Society.[24]

Fuller learned that Booth had known John Thomas and his relatives in his early days, and that he had considered him at one time "too wild and enthusiastic to be accepted for baptism."[25] In spite of this evident careless and erratic manner, Thomas did maintain an occasional contact with the Baptists. Serious financial difficulties, it seemed, caused him

---

21   S. Pearce Carey, *William Carey* (London: The Carey Press, 1934), 113.
22   "Our Theological Colleges. (1) In England", *The Baptist Quarterly*, 1 (1922–1923):20.
23   "Minutes of the Particular Baptist Society for Propagating the Gospel Among the Heathen" in John Rippon, *The Baptist Annual Register*, 1 (1790–1793):485.
24   Carey, *William Carey*, 104.
25   Kevan, *London's Oldest Baptist Church*, 124.

to take a position as surgeon on one of the ships of the East India Company. Following this period of service he returned to London by the close of 1784.[26] Supplementary accounts reveal that Thomas was converted by Stennett and baptized by Booth,[27] and that he was baptized in Soho Chapel, on Christmas Day. Thomas tried to set up in practice again and expressed the desire to become a minister. Again Booth, joined by Stennett, placed restraining hands on the young man. Together they dissuaded him from a hasty decision.[28]

Returning to Bengal, John Thomas studied and worked there for five years, learning Bengali and beginning Sanskrit, with the purpose of giving himself to evangelizing.[29] In 1792, the year the Society was organized, he came back to London and renewed his friendship with Stennett, Booth, and others, seeking their aid in establishing an Indian mission.[30] He still laboured under the handicap of the unfavourable impression he had given these conservative pastors.

A singular coincidence converted Booth into a warm advocate of the Indian mission proposal. Thomas was visiting Booth when Rev. John Campbell, afterwards a distinguished missionary to Africa, came in. In the course of the visit, the topic of conversation turned to Malda, and Campbell asked Thomas if he ever heard of a Mr. Thomas, a surgeon who had been preaching to the natives in India. Campbell explained that he had heard about his work through one of the bishops in Scotland, who had received enthusiastic reports from a friend in Malda. Thomas, to the surprise of Campbell, identified himself as the surgeon. Booth's hesitation was removed by this unexpected corroboration of Thomas' reports, and "he became from that time forward a strenuous supporter of the missionary cause," being the one who recommended Thomas to the new Society.[31]

At the next meeting of the committee on January 9, 1793, Fuller's findings were presented, and the following statements concerning their acceptance of Thomas are recorded in the minutes:

---

26 Ernest A. Payne, *The First Generation* (London: Carey Press, 1936), 69–70.
27 W.T. Whitley, *A History of British Baptists* (London: Kingsgate Press, 1932), 252.
28 Payne, *First Generation*, 69–70.
29 Whitley, *History*, 252.
30 Payne, *First Generation*, 71.
31 John Clark Marshman, *The Life and Times of Carey, Marshman, and Ward* (London: Longman, Browne, Green, Longmans, and Roberts, 1859), 1:51.

That they had received a satisfactory account of him. After all the information that could be obtained on Mr. Thomas's late labours in India were communicated, it was Resolved, that there appears to be an open door for preaching the gospel to the Hindoos—that, from what we have heard of the character, principles, abilities, and success of Mr. Thomas, a union with him in this important business is desirable; and That should Mr. Thomas accede to the Proposal, the Committee will endeavour to provide him a companion.[32]

That evening, Thomas arrived, accepted the invitation happily and joined forces with William Carey of Leicester, who was also present. He agreed to go out in the spring.

Andrew Fuller discloses further evidence that Booth was in full sympathy with the mission enterprise. Thomas and Carey were ready to embark; passage had been arranged when Carey's wife and her sister suddenly decided to go. The Society lacked £200 for their passage and had no time to raise it through the churches before his ship was scheduled to sail. Fuller immediately wrote to Newton, Booth, and Rippon. He told them of the situation and asked that they advance the money which, he assured them, could be immediately repaid.[33] It is recorded that "Mr. Booth and Dr. Rippon cheerfully assisted to the full extent of their credit,"[34] until the Society could reimburse them.

Abraham Booth corresponded closely with both Carey and Thomas. Two examples will suffice. On December 6, 1794, Thomas writes Booth:

> ...you will shortly hear of our pursuing our original plan, with more activity than we have been able hitherto; and us both hope to become helpers of our good society, rather than burthens. We often speak together of your kindness to us on leaving England; ...[35]

Carey's letter to Booth from Mudnabatty, on November 23, 1796, reads in part:

---

32 "Minutes of the Particular Baptist Society" in Rippon, *Baptist Annual Register*, 1:485.

33 John Ryland, *The Life and Death of the Rev. Andrew Fuller* (Charlestown: Samuel Etheridge, 1818), 139.

34 Marshman, *Life and Times*, 1:59.

35 *Periodical Accounts Relative to the Baptist Missionary Society*, 1 (1800):119.

Your very affectionate letters have been as cordials to my soul. Your counsels, your prayers, and good wishes excite my gratitude; may they be long continued![36]

Correspondence, at home between Booth and Andrew Fuller and others, shows him to have been in the very centre of things in these early years. The committee was called upon to consider the application of the beloved young pastor, Samuel Pearce, to join Carey in India in a letter dated November 3, 1794. Regarding this valuable man's desire, Booth counselled, "I cannot by any means encourage his going abroad as a missionary..." (although Booth believes) "the turn of his heart to be strongly for promoting the honour of Christ., &c."[37] The committee refused Pearce's request only because he could not be spared to the Society at home.[38]

Problems arising with launching the work in India caused a crisis in the ranks of the Society and its supporters at home. Because of inadequate support, extreme difficulties in gaining a foothold, and their previous understanding on the subject with the Society, Carey and Thomas took on outside employment. Thomas informed Booth in a letter, dated December 6, 1794, that Mr. Udney of Malda had given them charge of his indigo works.[39] A storm of protest arose over the "kind" of employment and its secularizing influence on the missionaries' minds. The committee sought the counsel of the London Baptist Ministers, by whose "strong language" they were "almost overset" for a time.[40] Booth called a meeting of Timothy Thomas, Dore, Keene, and Giles to discuss the matter, and, in a letter to Andrew Fuller, on March 30, 1795, he summarized their judgement under eight points. All of them signed the statement.

In short, their opinions are: Carey and Thomas have cut themselves off from the Society by their secular employment; they strongly disapprove of Thomas' discharging his own debts from public funds; the Society is now without a missionary at all; they would turn down "Mr. B's" offer (may be Thomas Blundel of Arnsby); they agree that

---

36 *Periodical Accounts*, 1:147.

37 "Calendar of Letters, 1742–1831", *The Baptist Quarterly*, 6 (1932–1933):218.

38 T.E. Fuller, *A Memoir of the Life and Writings of Andrew Fuller* (London: J. Heaton & Son, 1863), 217.

39 "Calendar of Letters", 219.

40 Fuller, *Memoir*, 105.

another mission should be started, and recommend Africa; and for avoiding prejudice against missions, they suggest that as little notice as possible be taken of the Carey and Thomas affair.[41] In the letter, Booth indicated that he agrees with the above opinions, unless Carey has some reasons for his conduct of which he is not aware. He is against sending any other person to the Indian mission at present, but he refers to the report of the Sierra Leone director and thinks two should be sent there. He agrees with Dr. Ryland that if two ministers cannot be found for that work, one minister and a private instructor or schoolmaster might be sent.[42]

The Society weathered this crisis, arising over the missionaries' employment, and Fuller, writing to Carey in August 1796, said, "You may think we have treated the Londoners with too much tenderness," but, he concluded, there is no cause to judge any man an enemy until he proves that he is one. Evidently he referred to Booth and Timothy Thomas, for he then went on to assure Carey that these two *remained* the Society's cordial friends. In a recent attempt, Mr. Swain and other young London ministers had tried to establish an assistant Society in London, but Booth and Thomas opposed it, saying, "If the Londoners form into a Society they will perhaps, have an ascendancy in the management; you have hitherto conducted the business well, and should it come under other influence?" Booth also managed successfully to conciliate Swain and his friends in the affair.[43]

In 1799, the Marshmans, Mr. Brunsdon, and Mr. Grant, the first group of reinforcements, went to the Indian mission. *The Periodical Accounts* narrates their departure:

> ...the missionaries accompanied by Mr. Fuller set off for London. There they met with their brethren from Bristol, and presently felt themselves to be of one heart, and of one soul. It was expected that the ship would sail in a few days, but it being detained in the harbour beyond the time, opportunity was afforded for a public meeting in London; and which was held at Mr. Booth's place of worship, on Friday, May 10. Brethren Thomas Thomas, Timothy Thomas, and Button, engaged in prayer, and Mr. Booth addressed the missionaries at their own request, and in a very serious and suitable manner, on the interesting, honourable, and arduous nature

---

41 "Calendar of Letters", 219–220.
42 "Calendar of Letters", 220.
43 "Calendar of Letters", 105–106.

of their undertaking. The London Brethren were much interested in the work, and carried it very affectionately to the missionaries.[44]

Financial support of the enterprise ran through private subscription, as far as possible and the gradual enlistment of whole church congregations. The *Periodical Accounts* annually published the lists of subscribers, and from the beginning of the work to the end of Booth's life, his name appears on these lists, along with a good number of Little Prescott Street members, two of his sons, and many additional large gifts under the title, "Anonymous from A. Booth."

Doubtless Abraham Booth did more to further the cause of foreign missions than is shown in the preceding paragraphs. Evidence which may be mentioned here and more fully discussed in connection with his writings, is the influence that his published works exerted on Adoniram Judson. In the preface to his statement of his change of sentiments from Congregationalism to the Baptist position of baptism of adult believers, Judson acknowledges his great debt to Booth's *Paedobaptism Examined*.[45] This change of conviction gave America its first Baptist foreign missionary and was directly responsible for the organization of the American Baptist Missionary Society.[46]

ABRAHAM BOOTH AND HOME MISSIONS

Before the century ended, seven men had been sent to Bengal and two to Sierra Leone, and the conscience of the Baptists had been awakened to the heathen in England. At the September 16, 1795 meeting of the Baptist Mission Society in Birmingham, a proposal was made for extending Society assistance for the encouragement of village preaching in England. It was revealed in the discussion that many people objected to giving to the support of missionaries in a foreign land so long as so many heathen remained at home. It appeared, however, that there was considerable interest in home mission work inspired by the foreign mission program, entirely apart from the complainers.

44   "An Address from the Committee of the Baptist Missionary Society to the Missionaries. May 7, 1799", *Periodical Accounts Relative to the Baptist Missionary Society*, 1 (1800):520.

45   Adoniram Judson, *A Sermon on Christian Baptism* (Boston: Bould, Kendall and Lincoln, 1846), 1.

46   H. C. Conant, *The Earnest Man: A Memoir of Adoniram Judson, D.D.* (London: J. Heaton and Son, 1861), 59 ff.

At the June 27, 1796 meeting of the Society, two men, Steadman of Broughton and Saffery of Salisbury, were approved and sent out for about ten weeks of itinerant preaching in the county of Cornwall. Extracts from their journals show that they held services in Baptist, Methodist, and Independent churches, private homes, in and under town halls, market houses, backyards, streets, at the horse-block, the pit, the Assize Hall, in meadows, an orchard, and an inn yard. Crowds ranging from thirty or forty to over 1,000 attended the efforts of these men. The home missionaries paid tribute to John Wesley's endeavours in the county, but concluded that something more permanent should be attempted, since temporary and sporadic work is of little permanent value.[47]

A year later, in 1797, Abraham Booth backed the organization of the "Baptist Society in London for the Encouragement and Support of Itinerant Preaching." John Rippon gives some basic information on the formation of the Society, publishing the rules covering constitution and activity. It was to be made up as follows:

> The following Ministers, Abraham Booth, John Martin, John Rippon, William Smith, William Button, James Dore, Timothy Thomas, Thomas Thomas, and Thomas Hutchings, with any other Baptist Ministers they may think proper, shall be considered as members, who, together with one member, being a subscriber, of each of their churches, and eleven others, whether members of churches, or not, chosen from among the subscribers at large; shall form a Committee, for conducting the affairs of the Society. This Committee shall meet in the afternoon of the day of each monthly association; five of whom shall be deemed sufficient to transact business.[48]

William Fox, the Little Prescott Street deacon, was elected treasurer, and Abraham Booth drafted the first appeal of the Society calling for suitable volunteers,

> …not merely to propagate a set of theological sentiments, though ever so true, much less to disseminate political opinions, or to canvas the affairs of state; but in the fear of God, with much prayer, circumspection and self-denial, to warn sinners of the wrath to come, to preach the unsearchable

---

47 "Efforts of the Society of the Propagation of the Gospel at Home", *Periodical Accounts Relative to the Baptist Missionary Society*, 1 (1800):262–263.

48 "The Baptist Society in London for the Encouragement and Support of Itinerant Preaching" in John Rippon, *The Baptist Annual Register*, 2 (1794–1797):469.

riches of Christ, and to render their ungodly fellow-creatures truly wise, holy, and happy.[49]

The organization's name was later changed to The Home Mission Society, and it is the oldest of the three societies which now comprise the Baptist Union of Great Britain and Ireland.[50] Some idea of the organization's growth is indicated by the report that by 1835 it was employing 100 full-time missionaries.[51] In March 1845, the income reported for the year ending that date was £4,981. 13s. 8d.[52]

That Booth was deeply concerned with the missionary cause is supported by the following opinion:

> The doctrines of Sovereign Grace are sometimes disparagingly spoken of as stunting evangelical endeavour. Let it be noted that this was a man who, maintaining and preaching those same doctrines, combined with them an outstanding evangelical zeal. He was a practical illustration of how these doctrines provide the very impetus to gospel enterprise.[53]

BOOTH'S CLOSING YEARS AND DEATH

Throughout most of his thirty-seven years of London ministry, Abraham Booth was blessed with good health and a strong constitution. He was described as having a muscular frame, never inclined to corpulence, but when he neared sixty, he suffered increasingly with asthma, particularly during the winter.[54]

A letter in the possession of Percy Stock of Shadwell, dated February 14, 1799, published in *The Baptist Quarterly*, presents an unusual impression of the unassuming pastor by an "Admirable Crichton, in buckled shoes, velvet knee breeches, and swallow-tailed coat" from the Barnoldswick Church: "Last Sabbath I heard Mr. Booth, he appears to greater advantage in writing than in the pulpit. He is rather in danger of a decline. So plain was his appearance that I mistook him before he

---

49   Quoted Seymour J. Price, *Upton: Story of One Hundred and Fifty Years 1785–1935* (London: The Carey Press, 1935), 17–8.

50   Kevan, *London's Oldest Baptist Church*, 123.

51   Robert G. Torbet, *A History of the Baptists* (Philadelphia: The Judson Press, 1950), 109.

52   Thomas Pottenger, "Progress and Present Numbers of the English Baptists", *The Baptist Memorial and Monthly Record*, 5 (1846):50.

53   Kevan, *London's Oldest Baptist Church*, 125.

54   "Memoir of the Author" (*Works*, 1:lix–lx).

ascended the rostrum for a poor layman."[55]

Though his health prevented his visiting his relatives and friends in Nottinghamshire during his latter years, Booth displayed a continuing and close interest in them through correspondence. A letter to his brother, Robert, on December 5, 1800, reads in part as follows:

> Dear Brother, I here send you an Old Great Coat for Uncle Elias Bradley. If, however, you think he has no occasion for it, you may give it to William Alleyn, or any other person whom you may consider as having the most need.
>
> I should be glad to be informed by you, the first opportunity, whether you think Uncle Elias stands in present need of assistance, for it would be our sin and our shame to suffer him to want the necessaries of life.
>
> Should be glad of information, how it is with the labouring poor; what are the prices of Provisions; and what your Parish rates are to the Poor. Should be glad to hear, whether you think Sister Morrell is comfortably situated at Grantham…
>
> How goest the cause of religion at your meeting, & among the Baptists at Sutton?[56]

Thomas Coles was secured for about six weeks to assist Booth during an illness in the winter of 1801. Apparently the pastor did not recover sufficiently for the church to consider him able to continue without an assistant and on March 22, the Minutes record the following:

> Agreed, That on account of our Pastor's confirmed Asthmatic Complaint, and advanced Age, it seems expedient he should have a Stated Assistant in the Public Ministry.[57]

This is the first record of his failing health. Coles was invited, and accepted the position as stated assistant. When he left to succeed Benjamin Beddome at Bourton on the Water, the church secured William Gray who remained as assistant pastor until Booth's death.

One of the greatest services Booth rendered in his later years was to the young ministers in his congregation, his assistants, and to other young men in and about London who sought his advice and assistance.

---

55 "Nathan Smith, to Barnoldswick, 1799", *The Baptist Quarterly*, 6 (1932–1933):232.

56 "Robert Booth of Kirkby Woodhouse", *The Baptist Quarterly*, 5 (1930–1931), 232-233.

57 Quoted Kevan, *London's Oldest Baptist Church*, 105, from Little Prescott Street Church Minutes.

His influence in the life of William Newman, the young pastor at the Old Ford Church, who became the first president of Stepney Academy, serves to illustrate. Newman's copious diary records that they met in 1792, apparently while Newman lived at Waltham Abbey, and they began corresponding, with Newman constantly seeking friendly advice from the venerable Booth. In one letter he says, "Pray, dear sir, do indulge me with a line or two, if you are not too much engaged. You know what it is to be a young christian, a young preacher."[58] In another, he writes, "May I take the liberty of requesting a few lines, elucidating the last part of I Peter iv.1 ..."[59]

There are frequent references in Newman's *Memoir* to Booth's counsel in study methods, personal attitudes, and ministerial deportment. One Sunday, in connection with his preaching, Newman wrote, "Lord, give me what my dear friend Booth wished me lately—liberty, with humility."[60] In a longer entry in his diary, we find an account of an afternoon spent with him. The pastor told him of the evening, seven or eight years previous, when, as he sat at home, he became impressed with the thought that he had never devoted one whole day to reading his Bible, although he had spent many a day reading human authors. This realization shamed him, and he determined, if the Lord permitted, that he would read nothing else until he had read his Bible. In three weeks he covered both the Old and the New Testaments and the Apocrypha. Following the telling of this experience, Booth advised his young friend to read a series of chapters connected on a particular subject, for instance, on the Sinai Covenant, from Exodus 19 to the end of Deuteronomy. Booth himself consulted his Hebrew Bible now and then, but he was a "smatterer." He began each day, however, with the reading of a chapter in his Greek Testament. By this method, before his death, he had read it some fifty times.[61]

After one of the monthly meetings of the London Baptists, Newman wrote in his diary: "Spent an hour with Mr. Booth; cautions against enthusiasm in applying promises. He said there was no promise in all the Bible that would ascertain that he should not die in a workhouse."[62] Nearer the end of Booth's life, Newman records: "Visited Mr. Booth,

---

58   Pritchard, *Memoir*, 56.
59   Pritchard, *Memoir*, 65.
60   Pritchard, *Memoir*, 69.
61   Pritchard, *Memoir*, 77–78.
62   Pritchard, *Memoir*, 154.

who is but very poorly. He thinks Mr. Hall, of Cambridge, in parts and learning, the first man in our denomination."[63]

A little later, Booth revised a short work on communion for Newman, and it was published in 1805 under the title of *Baptism, an Indispensable Term of Communion*.[64] His counsel on almost every matter of personal life and pastoral ministry found rich soil in Newman; his ministry at Old Ford flourished; and the unconscious preparation of Newman for his presidency of Stepney Academy continued. Newman purchased a part of Booth's library and spent considerable time in the presence of the great man discussing his publications.[65]

Joseph Ivimey, who later became an honoured minister and author, was another young man who had the coveted privilege of a close association with Booth in his closing days. Ivimey recorded bits of his experience:

> It was the privilege of the writer to become acquainted with this excellent minister about a year and a half before he was called to his reward. He hopes never to forget his affectionate counsels, and he has a strong and lively recollection of the ardent piety evinced, while he laboured under the violence of an asthmatic complaint. "I have never," said he, "thought so much of the words of Daniel to Belshazzar, as since I have been thus afflicted, 'the God in whose hand thy breath is!'... I trust I can say, to the honour of divine grace which has assisted me, that since I first professed religion, I have been so much preserved from every evil way, that if the secrets of my life were written by one who was not an enemy to me, there would be nothing to tell the world of which I should be ashamed to hear."[66]

Ivimey describes Booth's style of living as being most economical, recalling that he once dined with him in the kitchen on a plain meal. This mode of housekeeping enabled him to be "given to hospitality." When counselling Ivimey to economy in living on the income of a minister Booth told him:

> I have got some money by publishing my writings; but nothing, depend on it, for what I have published for the use of the Baptists. I have had some few legacies, but none amounting to more than one hundred pounds. I have

---

63 Pritchard, *Memoir*, 168.
64 Pritchard, *Memoir*, 179.
65 Pritchard, *Memoir*, 180.
66 Ivimey, *History*, 4:369.

put my children to boarding school; and had at times, a dozen of wine in my house; but never have I been able to do either at my own expense out of my income as a minister. If you do not take care, my friend, you will spend twenty pounds a year at your tea table.[67]

Although Booth continued as active as his strength would permit him until his death, a collection of personal letters in the possession of Dr. E.A. Payne give a graphic account of the state of his mind and body in his closing days. On June 19, 1804, Booth wrote his brother, William, at Annesley Woodhouse:

> In the late winter I preached but little nor did I expect to have survived the winter. Now, however, through divine goodness I appear in the pulpit once every Lord's Day. But having lately finished the seventieth year of age and my asthma increasing as my age advances, there is no reason to suppose that I shall survive another winter. Well, be that as it may, if I do but live to Christ while I am in the world I shall have little reason to be anxious about the time of my continuance here.[68]

Eight days before his death, he wrote again to William, thanking him for "a brace of hares sweet and good," and reporting that he hadn't been able to preach for some time but continued to attend services as a private worshipper, sitting beside the fire in the vestry. He continued:

> This week, however, I have been and still continue to be so much worse, that unless I be better on the next Lord's day I must probably keep at home. My respiration is more labourious, my cough more frequent and my strength less, all which connected with the idea of my being in the seventy-second year of my age, imperiously urge the necessity of considering myself on the verge of the grave. Diligently examine, Brother, the state of your heart, with regard to spiritual things....[69]

His final letter to his brother was written five days before his death:

Dear Brother,

Once more I take up my pen to send you a line before I leave this present

---

67 Ivimey, *History*, 4:377.
68 Abraham Booth, Manuscript Letter, Collection of Dr. E.A. Payne.
69 Abraham Booth, Manuscript Letter, Collection of Dr. E.A. Payne.

evil world; but am in full expectation of quitting my earthly tabernacle in a little while. I am become very feeble, and my respiration is labourious both night and day. It is with difficulty I can engage for a few minutes morning and evening in family prayer. I am scarcely fit for any employment of either body or mind. My life is so nearly run out that scarcely anything besides the drop remains. I have reason however to be unspeakably thankful; for I have a hope of eternal life. Yes, and old sinner as I am, all imperfect in my best services, and absolutely unworthy of any spiritual blessings, as I certainly am; I have hope of beholding the glory of Christ, and of being forever with him. Oh that I may bear with patient submission, and complete resignation, every application which yet awaits me and be helped to finish my course with joy. Forget not, Brother, that you also are an old man, and hastening to the end of life. Remember that the present life is the seed time of an eternal harvest. This is a very solemn thought. Oh! that it may rest upon your mind and operate more fully in your conduct! May you live as bordering on the grave and be prepared to depart at any time.

Yours affectionate &c.
Abrm. Booth
London
22nd Jany. 1806[70]

Five days later, at about nine o'clock, on the night of January 27, 1806, Booth died in the presence of Gray, his assistant pastor, and Granger, his son-in-law.[71]

His death called forth impressive tributes from both his friends and the press. A memorial in the church's records gives the facts of his death, with an account of the thirty-seven year period of service to the Little Prescott Street Baptist Church; his last sermon in September the previous year; the celebration of the Lord's Supper on the first Sunday in 1806; his attendance at the Monthly Baptist Meeting on January 23, 1806; and the fact that a large portion of his congregation visited him on the day before his death. Then follows a eulogy in glowing terms to Booth the man and Booth the minister.[72]

William Newman wrote in his diary, "This evening, my ever to be lamented friend, Mr. Booth, died; … He was the best friend, in some

---

70 Abraham Booth, Manuscript Letter, Collection of Dr. E.A. Payne.
71 "Memoir of the Author" (*Works*, 1: lxix).
72 "Memoir of the Author" (*Works*, 1: lxxx).

respects, I had on earth."[73] Almost all the religious periodicals published sketches of his life. *The Evangelical Magazine* gave an obituary notice and later a short memoir by John Rippon, introduced with the statement, "We have seldom, if ever, been called upon to record, in this Miscellany, a departed saint and minister of more sterling worth than the late Rev. Abraham Booth."[74] It also contained an epigram of twenty-five lines, upon Booth, written by "Mr. M_____ [Mackenzie], a well-known Portrait Painter, after having indefatigably exerted himself in producing a likeness of his departed Friend, Abraham Booth."[75]

An American magazine made some highly appreciative statements in an obituary notice of Booth:

> This apostolic servant of the Lord terminated his career in tranquility and Christian joy; and of him it may be fairly said, in honour of the grace of God, that viewed in all his characters, in his family, in his church and in the world; in his learning, in his influence, and in his piety, he was truly eminent.[76]

The deacons of the Little Prescott Street Baptist Church were instructed by the church to order a monument to the memory of Abraham Booth which was placed near the vestry door. As the church moved, the tablet accompanied it successively to Commercial Street and to the present Church Hill chapel, Walthamstow.[77] The inscription on this tablet reads in part:

> As a man, and as a Christian, he was highly and deservedly esteemed: As a Minister, he was solemn and devout: His addresses were perspicuous, energetic and impressive: they were directed to the Understanding, the Conscience, and the Heart. Profound Knowledge, sound Wisdom, and unaffected Piety, were strikingly exemplified in the Conduct of this excellent Man. In him, the poor have lost a humane and generous Benefactor; the Afflicted and the Distressed, a wise and sympathetic Counsellor; and this Church, a disinterested, affectionate, and faithful Pastor: nor will his name, or writings be forgotten, while Evangelical Truth shall be revered, Genius admired, or integrity respected.[78]

---

73 Pritchard, *Memoir*, 180.
74 "Memoir of the Late Rev. Abraham Booth", *The Evangelical Magazine*, 14 (1806):288.
75 *The Evangelical Magazine*, 14 (1806):336.
76 "Obituary", *The Massachusetts Baptist Missionary Magazine*, 1, No. 9 (February, 1807), 288.
77 Kevan, *London's Oldest Baptist Church*, 106.
78 "Memoir of the Author" (*Works*, 1: lxxx).

Perhaps the eulogy that would have been most pleasing to Booth himself was the advice he gave to the sinner in his own *Reign of Grace*:

> Be it your constant endeavour that, whenever your fair, your glorious, your heavenly Bridegroom shall come, he may find you ready; having your loins girt, your lamp burning, and waiting for his glorious advent. So shall your soul be peaceful, your life useful, and your death triumphant.[79]

William Jones of Liverpool prepared an essay on the life and writings of Abraham Booth which was published in 1808. A reviewer of Booth's collected works evaluates this memoir as a "meager sketch, miserably eked out … not worthy of the character of Abraham Booth."[80]

Dr. William Newman, recognizing the need for a better work, entered in his diary in 1826 a resolution to write a volume of reminiscences of Abraham Booth, with a review of his publications. In 1827, he wrote to Mr. Wayland, a grandson of Booth who had graduated from Stepney Academy in 1821, telling him he longed for retirement particularly to prepare a better account of Abraham Booth than had yet appeared. He had a few valuable manuscripts at the time and asked for Wayland's help in assembling others.[81] Evidently Newman did not find his opportunity to prepare this work for no full biography is extant.

---

79 Abraham Booth, *The Reign of Grace, From its Rise to its Consummation* (Philadelphia: Joseph Whetham, 1838), 333–4.

80 "Account of Religous Publications", *The Baptist Magazine* 6 (1814):164.

81 Pritchard, *Memoir*, 353.

John Calvin

*A sixteenth-century Reformer who stood at the fountainhead of the
theological tradition that Booth espoused during most of his life*

5

BOOTH THE CALVINIST

Eighteenth-century Particular Baptists, influenced by England's Great Awakening and aware of the stultifying effect of hyper-Calvinism, faced the problem of reconciling the duty of preaching and winning the unconverted, with the conviction that God has eternally chosen the particular persons who shall be saved. Abraham Booth, John Rippon, and Joseph Ivimey, all London pastors who had come to the city from rural districts, took the lead in leavening the high-Calvinism they found in the churches of the British capital.[1]

Abraham Booth's early experience with the General Baptists, who shared the ardent evangelism of the Moravians and Methodists,[2] could not be dismissed when he intellectually made the transfer from Arminianism to Calvinism, after a study of predestination. The years of warm, soul-saving experiences rang too true for Booth to abandon the means of preaching and seeking, even though his convictions were turned to a support of the doctrine of election. The latter was due to a study of the Scriptures, prayer, and probably the works of various writers on the subject, although he makes no mention of these. He held that "[h]owever firmly we may believe the existence of eternal decrees...we never suppose that those everlasting purposes...were designed to supersede the use of means."[3]

---

1   W.T. Whitley, *Calvinism and Evangelism in England, Especially in Baptist Circles* (London: Kingsgate Press, 1933), 1.

2   Whitley, *Calvinism*, 34.

3   Abraham Booth, *The Reign of Grace, From its Rise to its Consummation* (Philadelphia: Joseph Whetham, 1838), 68.

The Reign of Grace, published four or five years after his change of position, clarifies Booth's new stand and reveals that he did not carry his Calvinism to the extreme. On the doctrine of election, he stated:

> ...complete provision is made for the certain salvation of every sinner, however unworthy, who feels his want, and applies to Christ. The gospel is not preached to sinners, nor are they encouraged to believe in Jesus, under the formal notion of their being elected. No: these tidings of heavenly mercy are addressed to sinners considered as *ready to perish.*[4]

A further indication of his strong evangelistic bent is the unfailing invitation to sinners to read and consider their condition which accompanies every chapter of his published works and almost certainly every one of his preached sermons. In illustration:

> Remember, disconsolate soul, that the name, the nature, the office of grace enthroned, loudly attest, that the greatest unworthiness and the most profligate crimes are no bar to the sinner in coming to Christ for salvation; in looking to sovereign favor for all that he wants. Nay, they demonstrate, that the unworthy and sinful are the only persons with whom grace is at all concerned. This is amazing! This is delightful![5]

The record in the preceding chapter of Booth's initiating influence in a series of great missionary movements provides conclusive proof that he was evangelistic in practice. It now will be the purpose of this chapter to explore his doctrine, as it appeared in his published works and to prove the consistency of his Calvinism. Andrew Fuller and Robert Hall are repeatedly acknowledged as the moderators of the hyper-Calvinism of the Particular Baptists in England, bringing about a change in sentiment throughout the denomination, but it will be seen that Booth, who preceded their work by a very few years in his *Reign of Grace* and *Death of Legal Hope,* was pioneering along the same lines.

Booth's *Confession of Faith,* delivered at his ordination in 1769 and published with succeeding editions of *The Reign of Grace* presents the very core of his new Calvinism. This profession, with further and extensive supplement in *The Reign of Grace, Death of Legal Hope, Glad Tidings to Perishing Sinners, Divine Justice Essential to Divine Character,*

---

4   Booth, *Reign of Grace,* 63.
5   Booth, *Reign of Grace,* 23.

Thoughts on Dr. Edward Williams's Hypothesis Relative to the Origin of Moral Evil, and his prodigious works on baptism to be discussed in the next chapter, follows consistently the thirty-two articles of faith and practice, known as the *1689 Confession of Faith*, adopted by the Particular Baptists.

It is the writer's purpose to utilize the general outline of this famous old *Confession*, showing Abraham Booth's stand on the various points of doctrine, with necessary limitation to the basic issues despite the wealth of illustrative material his writings provide. Following a brief consideration of his individual works, the theology of Booth the man, will be examined. The natural divisions that his writings as a whole suggest, are Calvinism, baptism, and miscellaneous theological subjects, and that pattern will be followed in this and the succeeding chapter, with miscellaneous works appearing as Appendix I. Attention is called to the chronology at the beginning of the book, which details the principle events and publications of Booth; and also to Appendix II, "The Complete Works of Abraham Booth," listing all editions discovered in this research.

HIS CALVINISTIC PUBLICATIONS

The Reign of Grace. This work, which was produced in the early years of his connection with the Particular Baptists and published in 1768, is an exposition of Romans 5:21, "... even so might Grace reign, through righteousness, unto eternal life, by Jesus Christ our Lord." After defining and discussing the term "grace," Booth proceeds to develop the theme under the headings of grace reigning in our salvation in general, in election, calling, pardon, justification, adoption, sanctification, and perseverance. The closing part of the work concerns the Person of Christ, the work of Christ, from whom and by whom grace works, and the consummation of the reign of grace.

This work has been mentioned earlier in connection with Booth's change of sentiment, the London pastorate which it opened to him, and the favour the book has enjoyed through the years. It went through at least eleven editions, including a Dutch translation and four American editions, before the death of Booth, and its ministry continues to the present, forty-two editions having been discovered in the course of this research, including the latest, an American edition, in 1949.

Confession of Faith. Booth presented before the congregation of the Little Prescott Street Church at his ordination in 1769 this summary of his doctrinal stand. His statement acknowledged God, the divine Creator of all things, revealed in his creation and in the Godhead, Father, Son, and Holy Spirit; the Scriptures as God-inspired and the only rule of his faith and practice; man perfect as created but with free will which he exercised to disobey God, from whence all men are now by nature the children of wrath and dead in sin; Christ the atoning Saviour, crucified and risen; justification of sinners in the sight of God is purely, solely, entirely, by the righteousness of Christ imputed to them; regeneration of the sinner is absolutely necessary and only by divine agency, as also are faith and sanctification; Jesus Christ is the great Head of the church; baptism is immersion in water and is an emblem of the death, burial, and resurrection of Jesus; the Lord's supper is designed to impress the mind with a lively sense of the evil of sin; at death, the righteous immediately enter into glory and the evil into the abodes of darkness until the judgement day; resurrection of the dead, judgement, and eternal rewards.

The *Confession* closed with a pledge before Christ and the listening congregation that the statements he had made would be the guide and substance of his preaching and his ministry.[6]

The Death of Legal Hope. In 1770, the year after he was ordained, Booth published *The Death of Legal Hope, the Life of Evangelical Obedience*, an essay on Galatians 2:19. Following it by two years, *The Reign of Grace* seems to have been intended as a supplement to it, guarding that work from the extremes of Arminian legality and Antinomian licentiousness. He expressed the hope to his readers that, "you will take the happy medium—revere the law, as a transcript of the Maker's will and rule of your obedience to him."[7]

Booth set out to prove that until a sinner becomes dead to the law as a covenant of works and recognizes that he can never obtain acceptance with God through his own obedience, until he is brought to believe in Christ as the end of the law for righteousness, he cannot possibly live acceptably unto God. Grace is a doctrine producing godliness, not moral laxity.[8]

---

6 Booth, *Works*, 1:xxviii–xxxvii.
7 Booth, *Works*, 1:331–332.
8 Booth, *Works*, 1:335–437.

From the time Booth joined the Particular Baptists, he set himself to combat the Antinomianism toward which they tended, and he remarked to a friend, not long before his death, that if he were a young man, he would spend his life confuting the system of one particular, outstanding Independent preacher![9]

The Deity of Jesus Christ Essential to the Christian Religion. Socinianism was rife in the eighteenth century, and many of the clergymen of the Church of England even resigned their beneficences and cast their lot among the Dissenters of Socinian sentiments, because they could not conscientiously conform to Trinitarian worship. A formidable array of talent including Lindsey, Disney, Jebb, Wakefield, and Priestly, appeared on the side of the Socinians, attacking the orthodox belief.[10] The Trinitarians opposed them with strength, one of the ablest works being *The Deity of Jesus Christ Essential to the Christian Religion* by Dr. James Abbadie, Dean of Killaloe in Ireland. It was first written in French and later translated into English. In 1777, Booth was induced to present a new edition. His prefatory statement explained:

> The doctrine of our Lord's Eternal Divinity having been, on different grounds, the object of long and violent opposition; many learned, ingenious, and able pens have been engaged in defence of that capital truth. Few, however, have repelled the adversary with those powers of genius, and that force of argument, which were employed by Dr. Abbadie in composing this admirable Treatise.[11]

An English translation of this work had appeared many years before, but Booth revised, corrected, condensed, and concentrated the author's reasonings to the end that the value and usefulness were "much enhanced."[12]

R. Elliot is very critical of Booth's translation, however, calling it "too scholastic and obscure for common readers...subtle, overbearing, and evasive...not a clear reasoner...in some instances, a wrangler."[13] The work was published by subscription and received

---

9   "Memoir of the Author" (*Works*, 1:xli).

10   "Memoir of the Author" (*Works*, 1:xli–xlii).

11   James Abbadie, *The Deity of Jesus Christ Essential to the Christian Religion* (Burlington, N. J.: Thomas Ustick, 1802), ii.

12   "Memoir of the Author" (*Works*, 1:xlii).

13   R. Elliot, *The Consistent Protestant: or The Harmony of Divine Truth Asserted* (London, 1777), 36.

wide approval by members of the Church of England, as well as by his Dissenting brethren.[14]

Letter on the Arian Scheme. A letter regarding the Arian hypothesis, from Booth to a certain "Rev. E. S ... h of London," shows his concern for doctrinal purity among his fellow ministers. Booth listed eleven reasons why he could not embrace the Arian hypothesis, summarizing them as representing "Jesus Christ as neither God nor Man."[15] He concluded that Arianism represents Christ as a created God and an adorable man. It gives him the names and honours of God, but leaves him as dependent as a worm. He is either too high or too low, for as the Son of Man, he is the "super angelic excellence of mere humanity," and as the Son of God, he is "the first link in the immense chain of dependent beings" and is reduced to the size of a mere creature.[16]

Glad Tidings to Perishing Sinners. Differing opinions existed in the late eighteenth century as to the application of the gospel. All agreed that there must be a proper state of mind and spirit for its effective reception, but questions arose as to what constituted that proper state of mind. The sentiment, imported from America, was that regeneration consists wholly in a change of the will or heart, not of the intellect or understanding. The Spirit is the sole agent, and the gospel has no part. Those who have never been reconciled to God in any other way than by first seeing and believing in the grace of God through Christ, are yet ignorant of the true grace of God and enemies to it.[17]

In 1796, Booth published *Glad Tidings to Perishing Sinners; or The Genuine Gospel a Complete Warrant for the Ungodly to Belief in Jesus Christ*, in which he strongly opposed the above teaching, holding that it subverted the doctrine of divine grace in the justification of the ungodly. It made the gospel of no effect as a means of regeneration contrary to a long list of New Testament invitations to hear and accept it. His moderate Calvinism exerts itself strongly in his insistence that the New Testament teaches the great object of a gospel ministry is to hold forth the divine testimony to men of all sorts, and to give salvation to everyone that believes it. In fact, Booth went so far as to say that if regeneration precedes believing, men would be in a safe state without

---

14 "Memoir of the Author" (*Works*, 1:xlii).
15 "The Letter of the late Mr. Booth on the Arian Scheme", *The Baptist Magazine*, 2 (1810):62–66, 95–100.
16 "Letter of the late Mr. Booth", 100.
17 "Memoir of the Author" (*Works*, 1:li–lii).

coming to Christ.[18]

Andrew Fuller commented critically on this work, which resembles his own *Gospel Worthy of All Acceptation*, in a letter to John Ryland, in which he contended that Booth, all through his second chapter "confounds a warrant to come to Christ, with coming to him." Fuller held that a sinner may have a warrant to come to Christ, but if he is unwilling to exercise it, he cannot receive eternal life in his state of unwillingness. The objection that Fuller found to Booth's total denial of human merit was that, "one half of his reasonings are aimed, if they aim at anything, to prove that no holiness is necessary to coming to Christ, any more than to warrant our coming; and if so, faith must be an act of an ungodly mind."[19] As will be seen in a later discussion, these two Baptist leaders seem to have split on a fine line of disputation, but in basic doctrine, they were brothers.

Divine Justice Essential to Divine Character. In 1803, Booth published a work opposing the Socinian belief that when God inflicts penal evil upon the transgressor of his law, it is not because of any property in his nature that demands the punishment of sin, but because he is pleased to do so. Booth contends, as his title indicates, that it is essential to the perfection of divine character for God to punish creature-sin, and that he does it in wisdom and for his own glory. In the course of the essay, the subjects of imputation, substitution, and particular redemption are discussed, but Booth adds a considerable appendix in which he deals with these subjects more thoroughly.[20]

A controversy between Booth and Andrew Fuller resulted from this work, which Fuller interpreted as attacking his *Gospel Worthy of All Acceptation*. A more detailed report of the conflict will appear in the discussion of the atonement in the succeeding section.

Thoughts on Dr. Edward Williams's Hypothesis Relative to the Origin of Moral Evil. Booth replies to Williams in an essay published posthumously in 1813. He attacked the author's claim that rebellion is an absolutely necessary and inherent tendency in the creature. Williams's concept, as Booth saw it, was "a vast system of intelligences, every one of whom, from the first moment of his being, could not but have a tendency to renounce the dominion of his Creator, and to hate

---

18   Abraham Booth, *Glad Tidings to Perishing Sinners* (London, 1796), 2–162.

19   John Ryland, *The Life and Death of the Rev. Andrew Fuller* (Charlestown: Samuel Etheridge, 1818), 242.

20   Booth, *Works*, 3:3–95.

him for ever." To Booth, this hypothesis blasphemed against divine perfection and libeled the souls now residing in heaven. Evil's existence and prevalence are consistent with God's perfection, and his conduct in reference to evil will eventuate to the praise of his glory.[21]

THE STRUCTURE OF BOOTH'S THOUGHT

Booth did not attempt to set forth a complete system of theology as will be seen throughout this discussion. His preoccupation with the subjects of grace, election, and the atonement caused him to treat other doctrines with comparative brevity and simplicity. His failure to fully develop a theological system would seem to indicate his apparent satisfaction with the Calvinistic interpretations he followed.

Booth's *Confession of Faith* stated his dependence on the Bible as the sole authority for his faith and practice. To him, the Scriptures were their own spokesman for their divine origin, and in this *Confession* he enumerates the reasons for his own acceptance of them as God's revelation:

> The sublimity and spirituality of its doctrines...The purity of its precepts— The prophecies...The character of its penmen—The perfect harmony of design subsisting amongst them, and the grandeur of that design— Their unreserved freedom in relating matters of fact...the long series of uncontrolled miracles which were wrought in proof of its doctrines being divine.

With still other evidences of its power in the lives of men and the happenings of time, he finds it worthy in every way of its infinite Author.[22]

Booth encountered no problem in accepting the infallibility and complete authority of the Scriptures as the Word of God. His brief statement of his position did not discuss any of the theories of inspiration, and it is reasonable to assume that he followed Calvin in his belief that not every word of Scripture leads to faith, but that it is assuredly the Word of God.

The Trinitarian controversy reached its peak during the eighteenth century in England, with such writers as Leslie, Whiston, Robinson,

---

21 Booth, *Works*, 3:393–408.
22 "Confession of Faith" (*Works*, 1:xxix–xxx).

Wells, Potts, and Jones defending the orthodox position. Dr. Waterland ably contended with Dr. Clarke, and Dr. Horsley distinguished himself in opposing Priestly.[23] Abraham Booth made clear his own stand on the side of the triune God, stating, "…in the unity of the Divine Essence there are three distinct Persons, the Father the Son, and the Holy Ghost; [who] … must be one in essence and equal in glory, whatever inferiority there may be in respect to office in the economy of redemption."[24] His concept of the Father represented him as holding forth majestically and powerfully the rights of Deity, while his eternal Son, through his "amazing condescension," displayed with honour every divine perfection and "in his lowest state of subjection, could claim an equality with God."[25]

Booth's doctrine of the Trinity is largely confined to these statements from his two earliest writings, *The Reign of Grace* and his *Confession*. Perhaps his relative silence on the subject is explained by his translating James Abbadie's *The Deity of Jesus Christ Essential to the Christian Religion*, which represented his thinking on the subject without further need for elaboration. In the introduction to this work, Abbadie defended his own simple stand by saying, "We shall have no recourse to metaphysical speculations, to shew how the thing is; but we shall make it appear, from divine Revelation, that it really is."[26]

Booth's statements are too brief to touch upon either the psychological analogies of Augustine or the social analogies of the Cappadocian fathers in his speculative construction of the doctrine. Here again Abbadie answers for him:

> Many learned and pious men have laboured hard to find out pertinent similitudes, by which to illustrate a subject which is unsearchably deep and beyond all comparison. Such attempts, however well-intended, cannot fail of proving abortive, and are often injurious to the cause they were designed to serve.—These comparisons are not adapted to answer the end as they speak only to our imagination. Now it is not the *imagination*, but *reason* that must be satisfied.[27]

---

23   J. Abbey and J.H. Overton, *The English Church in the Eighteenth Century*, 197–224.
24   "Confession of Faith" (*Works*, 1:xxxi).
25   Booth, *Reign of Grace*, 281.
26   Abbadie, *Deity of Jesus*, 14.
27   Abbadie, *Deity of Jesus*, 310.

It may be concluded even on limited evidence from Booth and from Abbadie, that the Londoner accepted the Western doctrine of the Holy Spirit proceeding from the Father and the Son, as opposed to the Eastern or Greek belief that the Spirit proceeded from the Father alone.

Abraham Booth acknowledged his belief in the doctrines of original sin and the total depravity of man, asserting that in the fall of Adam, the natural and federal head of mankind, all his offspring sinned in him and fell with him, the guilt of his first sin being imputed.[28] Men do not suffer under Adam's offence merely by imputation, however, because his sin legally belongs to all who are of his nature and descent.[29]

Booth, in subscribing to the Augustinian theory of Adam's natural headship,[30] departed somewhat from Calvin's contention that God willed that all men since Adam should be so born.[31] He answered the objection to man's helplessness in the face of transmitted guilt in stating that man, by his federal relationship to Adam was involved in the first transgression before it was imputed to him, or it could not have been justly charged to him.[32]

> Hence it is that all men are by nature the children of wrath; averse to all that is spiritually good, and prone to evil; dead in sin, under the curse of the righteous law, and obnoxious to eternal vengeance. From which state of complicated misery, there is no deliverance but by Jesus Christ, the second Adam.[33]

In a period when Christ's position in the eternal plan was subjected to the widest variety of interpretation, from complete humanizing to total deification, Booth staunchly held to the Orthodox, or Chalcedonian (451 AD)[34] view of Christ as the Mediator, both God and man, eternally reigning on high and interceding for men. For Christ to deliver man, the transgressor, by his vicarious sufferings, it was necessary that he himself be man, derived from the root of Adam, yet conceived entirely without sin. He partook of the nature that knew sin, without sinning in the least

---

28 "Confession of Faith" (*Works*, 1:xxxii).

29 Booth, *Reign of Grace*, 278–279.

30 A.H. Strong, *Outlines of Systematic Theology* (Philadelphia: The Griffith & Rowland Press, 1908), 165–166.

31 See, for example, Calvin, *Institutes* 2.1.7.

32 Booth, *Reign of Grace*, 185.

33 "Confession of Faith" (*Works*, 1:xxxii).

34 Strong, *Outlines*, 181.

himself. He was God as surely as he was man.[35]

Christ's extreme sufferings, in comparison with other men who have endured deaths as physically agonizing as his, Booth saw as proof of their vicarious character. His substitutionary role, too, is the only logical explanation for the Father's conduct toward him in his sorrows. In his *Confessions* Booth summarized his concept of Christ's atoning work as follows:

> ...having all the sins of all his people imputed to him and charged upon him, he died the ignominious, the painful, the cursed death of the cross...a vicarious atoning sacrifice, for their sins, and to expiate their innumerable and enormous crimes. In these sufferings of the Son of God on the cross I behold, in the clearest light, the infinite evil of sin displayed, and the awful wrath of God revealed against it, the law magnified, Justice satisfied, and God himself was well-pleased...Jesus...arose from the dead the third day... he ascended triumphant to the right hand of the Majesty on high, where he shines and reigns the Incarnate God...king of Zion and ruler In his church; but also, as the God of providence and governor of the world:...a faithful intercessor.[36]

It is true that Booth's statement is crude and inadequate, but it was in keeping with that of Calvin, to whom he looked for much of his guidance. Before the end of the nineteenth century, R.W. Dale[37] and James Denney[38] presented much more pleasing restatements, as witness Denney's interpretation of the Person of Christ and the atonement:

> He is doing the will of God on our behalf, and we can only look on. It is the judgment and mercy of God in relation to our sins which we see in Him, and His Presence and work on earth are a divine gift, a divine visitation. He is the gift of God to men, not the offering of men to God, and gives Himself to us in and with Him. We owe to Him all that we call divine life. On the other hand, this divine visitation is made, and this divine life is imparted, through a life and work which are truly human. The presence and work of Jesus in the world, even the work of bearing sin, does not prompt us to define human and divine by contrast with each other: there is no suggestion of incongruity between them.

---

35 Booth, *Reign of Grace*, 278–281.
36 "Confession of Faith" (*Works*, 1:xxxii–xxxiii).
37 R.W. Dale, *The Atonement* (London: Congregational Union of England and Wales, 1888), 492–493.
38 James Denney, *The Death of Christ* (New York: A.C. Armstrong and Son, 1902), 317–318.

Booth did attempt to safeguard the Anselmic or objective element in the atonement, namely, that something objective was wrought here whereby the relation of God to man was mended, against the inroads of the Socinian Examplarist theory.

Modern theology has reacted vigorously against the liberal movement of the late nineteenth and early twentieth centuries, which stressed the moral theory of the atonement as set forth by Abelard, "Christ creating within us by His passion a love which itself delivers from sin."[39] The search, once more, is for an objective atonement in which the just claims of God and his judgement are made and in which the tyranny of sin is broken. Emil Brunner, in *The Mediator*,[40] undertakes such a statement, and we find P.T. Forsyth, in a more gracious way, safeguarding the objective element which the Calvinists, Booth included, stressed:

> The work of Christ was thus in the same act triumphant on evil, satisfying to the heart of God, and creative to the conscience of man by virtue of His solidarity with God on the one side, and on the other with the race. He subdued Satan, rejoiced the Father, and set up in Humanity the kingdom—all in one supreme and consummate act of His one person. He destroyed the kingdom of evil, not by way of preparation for the kingdom of God, but by actually establishing God's kingdom in the heart of it. And he rejoiced, filled, and satisfied the heart of God, not by a statutory obedience, or by one private to Himself. Which spectacle disposed God to bless and sanctify man; but by presenting in the compendious compass of His own person a Humanity presanctified by the irresistible power of His own creative and timeless work.[41]

Booth's later work, *Divine Justice Essential to Divine Character*, expresses his belief in divine justice as the central note of his doctrine of the atonement. He recognized the reality of sin and the judgement: the reality of God and his just and essential claim for payment of sin and the atonement as just and necessary for reconciliation.

Both the satisfaction and penal elements of the atonement are to be found in Booth, in a form that today is viewed as excessively

---

39 *Encyclopaedia of Religion and Ethics* (New York: Charles Scribner's Sons, 1910), 1:18.
40 Emil Brunner, *The Mediator* (Philadelphia: The Westminster Press, 1947), 516–535.
41 Peter Taylor Forsyth, *The Work of Christ* (New York: Hodder and Stoughton, 1938), 224–225.

transactional and mechanical.[42] His focusing on the twofold imputation of man's guilt imputed to Christ and his righteousness imputed to man,[43] is subject to criticism for almost ignoring the life and teachings of Jesus in its concentration upon his death. Dale, in his far more recent support of the penal theory, has been subjected to this same criticism.[44]

Booth's "Latin" view is in marked contrast with the "classic" theory of the atonement which Bishop Gustaf Aulen advanced, in the past quarter century, as a revival of the doctrine of the early church and of Luther. Aulen classifies the satisfaction and subjective theories as rationalized doctrines that provoked the Reformation and have continued the schism. His classic theory, briefly stated, is "A Divine conflict and victory; Christ—*Christus Victor*—fights against and triumphs over the evil powers of the world, the 'tyrants' under which mankind is in bondage and suffering, and in him God reconciles the world to Himself."[45]

In an Appendix to *Divine Justice*, Booth elaborated further on the doctrine of the atonement, particularly in connection with its application. He saw the atonement itself made solely by Christ, while the Holy Spirit makes its application. The atonement is objective but its application is a work done subjectively. The application can be known as "believing in Jesus," but it is not to be confused with the atonement itself.[46] In this distinction, he was taking to task Andrew Fuller with whom he sustained a controversy over the question of particular redemption. Fuller's position, in his *Gospel Worthy of All Acceptation* was that the atonement is *sufficient* for the salvation of the whole world, if the whole world were to embrace it, but is *particular* in connection with God's sovereign application of it.[47]

In his "Six Letters to Dr. Rye Respecting the Controversy with the Rev. A. Booth," Fuller lamented that he had tried for years to conciliate and satisfy Booth in his repeated attacks on his theology, but despite their mutual high regard, they continued to differ on minor points of their thinking. Fuller related to Ryland the position he had tried to make clear to Booth prior to the latter's printing of *Divine Justice Essential to*

---

42 T.H. Hughes, *The Atonement* (London: George Allen & Unwin Ltd., 1949), 32.

43 *Divine Justice* (*Works*, 3:54).

44 Hughes, *Atonement*, 82.

45 Gustaf Aulen, *Christus Victor* (New York: The Macmillan Company, 1945), 20.

46 *Divine Justice* (*Works*, 3:43).

47 *The Gospel Worthy of All Acceptation* in *The Complete Works of the Rev. Andrew Fuller* (Philadelphia: American Baptist Publication Society, 1845), 2:374.

Divine Character, only to find himself openly attacked, in the Appendix, on the original grounds of confusing a thing with its application.[48]

Fuller replied to Booth in a small work, *Three Conversations* in which the speakers were Peter (Booth), James (Fuller), and John, the moderator (Ryland). Their subjects were: "On Imputation," "On Substitution," and "On Particular Redemption." The material for the latter was lifted bodily from Booth's *Divine Justice*. It appears that the controversy was largely a debate on the force of certain terms and came to little consequence. "John," in a summary statement in the *Conversations*, concludes, "You are agreed in all the great doctrines of the gospel... The greater part of those things wherein you seem to differ may be owing to a difference in the manner of expressing yourselves...."[49]

Booth was in complete accord with Fuller on the limited atonement, which they both interpreted as limited in its application, but not in its sufficiency.

> There is no reason at all to wonder, that *He that spared not his own Son, but delivered him up* to the curse of the law, and the death of the cross, to make atonement for sinners; should take effectual care that the all sufficient atonement should be *applied* to every individual for whom at so vast an expence, it was made.[50]

In a final word on the atonement in his *Divine Justice*, Booth dealt with the problem involving God's attributes of justice and grace. The author saw the atonement as more truly the evidence of God's love to the sinner than the manifestation of his hatred to sin. It is not primarily the purity of God's nature that prompted the atonement, but the compassion of his heart; his determination to pardon sin is stronger than his inclination to punish.[51] Booth did not reveal an embarrassment over a tension existing within God, but he might be seen to agree with P.T. Forsyth in his statement that, "There can therefore be no strife of attributes."[52] Aulen speaks of this tension as resolved in the cross. Grace breaks through and triumphs over death.[53]

---

48 Ryland, *Life and Death*, 240–242.
49 "Three Conversations on Imputation, Substitution and Particular Redemption" (*Complete Works*, 2:501–528).
50 *Divine Justice* (*Works*, 3:87).
51 *Divine Justice* (*Works*, 3:90).
52 Forsyth, *Work of Christ*, 118.
53 Aulen, *Christus Victor*, 75–76.

Booth's *Reign of Grace* may be considered his masterpiece, and as shown earlier, it won him the recognition that lifted him from obscurity in Nottinghamshire, to the pastorate of London's most important Baptist church. He chose to give further substance to this work by the addition to the last corrected edition, of an entire chapter on election, "which renders the doctrines more complete, and the contents of the book more answerable to the title."[54] Booth's understanding of this doctrine of election motivated his change from General to Particular Baptist position and determined the role he was to play in moderating the extremes to be found in the latter position. The most succinct statement of his Calvinistic stand on election appears in his *Confession*:

> The eternal Sovereign, before the world began, of his own good pleasure, and to manifest the riches of his glorious grace, foreseeing the fall of man, chose a certain number of this apostate race to eternal salvation, whom he *predestinated to the adoption of children by Jesus Christ, according to his own sovereign will*; and, in pursuance of this grand and gracious design, he entered into a covenant of grace and peace with the Son of his love on their behalf, in which a Saviour was appointed, and all spiritual blessings provided for them.[55]

The end of election is God's glory, whether it is found in the complete salvation and endless happiness of some of his creatures or in the righteous condemnation of others. Sin is not permitted to subvert the grand design but is made subservient to it.[56]

It would appear that Abraham Booth was supralapsarian in sentiment, placing the decree of election before the decree to provide redemption.[57] His hyper-Calvinism on this matter, in establishing the supremacy of God's sovereign will (although Brunner argues this is not John Calvin's emphasis)[58] over all other considerations, he sought to justify by his claim that God's choice was based on *love*, in his selecting "a certain number out of the apostate race of Adam" to participate in grace on earth and glory hereafter.[59] Booth's statement that the love of

---

54 Booth, *Reign of Grace*, iii.

55 "Confession of Faith" (*Works*, 1:xxxii).

56 Booth, *Reign of Grace*, 26.

57 Heinrich Heppe, *Reformed Dogmatics* (London: George Allen & Unwin Ltd., 1950), 147.

58 Emil Brunner, *The Christian Doctrine of God. Dogmatics.* (London: Lutterworth Press, 1949), 324.

59 Booth, *Reign of Grace*, 27.

God is the dominant note of the scriptural atonement, is contended with considerably more emphasis by such modern writers as Forsyth, Denney, Lidgett, Mackintosh, Robinson, and Walker, reviewed in *The Atonement* by T.H. Hughes.[60]

Booth based his entire interpretation of election on the belief that men, "considered as guilty creatures deserve to perish forever."[61] His acceptance of the total depravity of man enabled him to pass over the question as to whether the damnation of any can give glory to God. He considered it blasphemy to suppose that God finds delight in human misery and declared the only end of election that satisfies reason or Scripture is God's own glory.[62] He reasoned that it is only just for those who disobey God's will to have to "honour him passively and perpetually" through their deserved sufferings. God's nature, in the light of his laws and his majesty, demands punishment for the crimes and apostasy of his rebellious creatures, but this punishment is deserved and just—not arising as the Socinians claimed, from his arbitrary practice of inflicting suffering merely because it pleased him to do so.[63]

> Does he execute vengeance on any of the works of his hands? it is to demonstrate the infinite opposition of all his perfections to moral evil, and for the honour of his eternal justice, as a righteous governor. Does he spare any of the rebellious subjects of his vast dominions, and, save them from the death they deserved? it is to display his mercy in connexion with truth and righteousness, and for the glory of all his unchangeable attributes.[64]

A little over a half century ago, Dr. Dale stated this uncompromising concept of punishment as: "the penalties of sin are primarily an expression of the principle that the sinner deserves to suffer."[65]

The system of double decrees set forth by Calvin,[66] cannot be identified positively in Booth. In his treatment of Romans 9:17–18, he passes over the double decree clauses, stressing only the sole cause of election as the sovereign pleasure of God and its end the glory of

---

60 Hughes, *Atonement*, xv.
61 Booth, *Reign of Grace*, 77.
62 Booth, *Reign of Grace*, 49.
63 *Divine Justice* (*Works*, 3:14–15).
64 Booth, *Reign of Grace*, 49.
65 Dale, *Atonement*, 378–379.
66 See, for example, Calvin, *Institutes* 3.21.

God.[67] C.H. Dodd and others see in Paul's argument here, a false step, holding that "it was not necessary for his argument to show that God also creates bad dispositions in those who are not to be saved."[68]

In the picture of God as the potter, exercising sovereignty over mankind, the clay, Booth saw an illustration of the Creator's free choice in designing different vessels for different purposes, irrespective of the nature of the clay. One part cannot dictate how it is to be formed any more than another. The potter's choice is assuredly righteous because Jehovah cannot be conceived as decreeing unwisely, governing without rectitude, or punishing without justice.[69] Apparently Booth thought it sufficient to stress the elect and leave the non-elect to divine justice. He would seem to be in agreement with the simple, spiritual stating of Emil Brunner that "the eternal election of God should always be spoken of only in correlation with faith."[70]

Booth recognized that this doctrine of election or distinguishing grace, in stripping away every vestige of human pride, leaving no difference between persons, and resolving the whole into divine grace and divine sovereignty, is "a tenet so unpolite," its professors must expect ridicule and reproach.[71]

The Arminian concept of universal redemption now appeared to Booth contrary to reason and revelation. He could not suppose that Christ would serve as Mediator for sinful men without knowing who, if anyone, would accept his sacrifice. Faith, as he saw it, was a gift of grace bestowed only on those whom God eternally determined should receive it. No new determinations come from God. His purposes come from everlasting, and he is unchangeable in his perfections.[72]

The author found his satisfaction to the question of why some were chosen and others not, in God's answer, "I will have mercy on whom I will have mercy" (Romans 9:15). He could acknowledge that all mankind is in sin, on a perfect level in the eyes of God. Christ gave his approbation to the Father's determination in his statement, "Even so, Father, for so it seemed good in thy sight."[73]

67   Booth, *Reign of Grace*, 43–44.
68   C.H. Dodd, *The Epistle of Paul to the Romans. The Moffett New Testament Commentary* (New York: Harper & Brothers Publishers, 1932), 157.
69   Booth, *Reign of Grace*, 47–49.
70   Emil Brunner, *The Divine-Human Encounter* (London: S.C.M. Press, 1944), 89.
71   Booth, *Reign of Grace*, 29.
72   Booth, *Reign of Grace*, 34.
73   Booth, *Reign of Grace*, 29.

Adhering firmly to the Calvinist position, Booth declared that faith in Christ and obedience are the fruits and effects of election, not the cause. There would be no need for election, he reasoned, if men could be seen to possess faith and holiness before they were chosen.[74]

This doctrine of election thus set forth, gives rise to gratitude and sacred love on the part of the elect, whose joyous expression is, "Jehovah has condescended to take me for his own: I choose him for my portion, I love him as my all."[75]

Booth's moderate Calvinism is seen in his reply to the objection that if one be not of God's elect, he is helpless no matter how much he desires to be saved. The author denies that there is any need for the sinner to "peruse the eternal roll of God's decrees and read his name in the book of life, before he can upon solid grounds apply to Christ for salvation." No sinner is required to prove his election before he is accepted, because God's Word gives every encouragement needed for the sinner who recognizes his perishing condition to rely completely on Christ for his pardon and peace.[76] Andrew Fuller elaborated on this same theme in his *Gospel Worthy of All Acceptation*:

> If God, through the death of his Son, has promised salvation to all who comply with the gospel and if there be no *natural* impossibility as to compliance nor any obstruction but that which arises from aversion of heart; exhortations and invitations to believe and be saved are consistent; and our duty, as preachers of the Gospel, is to administer them, without any more regard to particular redemption than to election ... [77]

On the other hand, the Antinomian who believes himself to be elected and indulges in spiritual indifference or moral looseness, is abusing the doctrine of grace and marks himself as a vessel of condemnation instead of an object of sovereign mercy.[78]

The way out of every theological difficulty, Booth resolved, as did Calvin, is by reproaching man for his high opinion of himself and his diminutive thoughts of his Maker. This misconception of man's position in relation to God caused him to rebel against God's sovereign will in

---

74 Booth, *Reign of Grace*, 37–38.
75 Booth, *Reign of Grace*, 59.
76 Booth, *Reign of Grace*, 63–64.
77 *Gospel Worthy of All Acceptation* (*Complete Works*, 2:374).
78 Booth, *Reign of Grace*, 64–66.

the matter of election. The author urged that the matter be submitted to "clear reason":

> … it is impossible to conceive how his choosing some to life and happiness, and his rejecting others, can afford the least occasion for the charge suggested in the objection. For the election of those whom God determined to save, does not injure the non-elect. Their situation would not have been at all the better, if none had been chosen, nor any saved. For non-election to not be a punishment; it is only the withholding a free favour, which the sovereign Lord of all may bestow on whomsoever he pleases.[79]

Following upon the doctrine of election, was Booth's consideration of effectual calling, the work of the Holy Spirit in leading the perishing sinner to the Father after he has received the invitation of grace in the gospel.[80] The Holy Spirit convinces man of sin by the law and brings him to the realization that he deserves divine wrath and the damnation of hell. He must face the fact that he is utterly helpless without Christ's propitiation for his sins, before he can seek or accept the atonement. Those who are too proud to rely entirely on sovereign grace must not be surprised if that grace does not assist them. "They appeal to the law, and by it they must stand or fall."[81] Booth's position on baptism, to be reviewed in Chapter 6, necessarily eliminates any consideration of the ordinance as an instrument of regeneration.

After a sinner has received his effectual calling, there is the question of justification which Brunner identifies as "the most incomprehensible thing that exists," with Christ taking our place and we taking his. Booth defined it as "no other than the way of a *sinners acceptance with God.*" Judiciously, but graciously, God absolves the sinner of his guilt, frees him from condemnation, and gives him the right to eternal life solely through Christ's obedience imputed to him and accepted by faith. Thus, "The Triune God justifies."[82] The Father appoints the way, and sends his Son to perform the conditions of acceptance. The Son makes the atonement, and the Holy Spirit reveals the Saviour's work to sinners, enables them to receive it, and testifies to them of their

---

79   Booth, *Reign of Grace*, 74–75.
80   Booth, *Reign of Grace*, 84–85.
81   Booth, *Reign of Grace*, 97.
82   Brunner, *Mediator*, 524.

complete justification.[83]

Booth affirmed that justification is accomplished by grace alone, as opposed to works. The one justified is judged in a state of complete unworthiness at the moment he is accorded the blessing of divine acceptance. The faith by which man is justified is in itself a gift of grace and not an element of man's own righteousness. Men are dependent upon a perfect obedience, either performed by them or imputed to them, since God does not accept anyone by any holiness existing within him even though wrought by the Holy Spirit.[84] It is apparent in Booth's body of doctrine that "evangelical faith" is "a dependance on Jesus alone for eternal salvation."[85] Grace, the dominant note of Booth's theological thinking, reigns supreme in man's salvation. The good pagan finds no grounds for justification other than as a sinner saved by grace. Borrowing the words of his friend, Henry Venn, Booth was careful to make it clear that "self sufficient moralists, and devout cheats, are criminals alike: that prayerless honest men, and hymn-singing villains, are much more nearly related, than either will choose to believe. For which cause the same perdition is reserved for hypocrites and unbelievers."[86]

God's gracious admission of strangers and aliens into the relationship of children, through Jesus Christ, is known as adoption and is a fulfillment of the promise that "I will be a Father unto you, and ye shall be my sons and daughters, saith the Lord Almighty" (2 Corinthians 6:18; 2 Samuel 7:14). Booth distinguished this doctrine from reconciliation, whereby the sinner and God are made friends, and justification, through which he is pronounced righteous. Adoption assures that he is now an heir of the eternal inheritance.[87]

Although his belief in election might have led him into a laxity of conduct, Booth considered sanctification as a blessed fulfillment of calling and justification. He defined it as the work of divine grace whereby God's heirs are renewed after his image. True holiness and a conformity to the moral perfections of God are its effect. Sanctification is progressive and is the end of election. It is a fruit of redemption, God's design in regeneration, "the primary intention of justification—

---

83 Booth, *Reign of Grace*, 149.

84 Booth, *Reign of Grace*, 158–177.

85 Booth, *Reign of Grace*, 192.

86 *Divine Justice* (*Works*, 3:71), quoted in Henry Venn, *Mistakes in Religion Exposed: An Essay on the Prophecy of Zacharia* (New York: Williams and Whiting, 1810), 192.

87 Booth, *Reign of Grace*, 203–204.

the scope of adoption—and absolutely necessary to glorification."[88]

Booth explained that the redeemed, in love, out of a pure heart, seek to please the Father, but are not in slavish fear of eternal wrath. "Though they may justly expect more copious manifestations of their Father's love, when they walk in obedience to him; yet they do not obey to obtain life, or to gain a right of inheritance. No, they are already heirs."[89]

Booth settled to his own satisfaction the eternal debate over the place of good works in the plan of redemption and in the life of the Christian by regarding works as highly necessary for showing forth the redeemed state but as of no value at all in justification or salvation. To avoid the fatal extremes of Arminian legality or Antinomian licentiousness, he urged: "We should therefore be exceedingly careful rightly to distinguish between the foundation of our acceptance with God, and that superstructure of practical godliness which must be raised upon it."[90] Although Christ provides absolute freeness, the conduct of his followers is the key to their true spiritual condition.[91]

The Death of Legal Hope, which, in effect, was a supplement to *The Reign of Grace*, deals extensively with the utility of works and the law. In illustration, Booth cited the Judaizers who relied on their own duties, considering themselves copartners with Jesus in obtaining salvation. In so doing, they *"became debtors to the whole law, and were obnoxious to its dreadful curse."* The Arminians, he suggested, are likened to them in their insistence upon supplementing the work of Christ and denying the complete efficacy of grace.[92]

The doctrine of the eternal perseverance of the saints, contented by the Arminians and Romanists, Booth supported with his statement that God's "love must abate, or his purpose rendered void before they [the saints] can finally fall." He argued that if one soul for whom Christ died should perish, then divine justice would be demanding double payment, a situation not to be countenanced.[93] Christ's example of fervent prayer despite the fact that his happiness and eternal reward were assured as Mediator, is an answer to the perversion of the doctrine, that as one is saved, he has no reason to live carefully. Although the

---

88 Booth, *Reign of Grace*, 215.
89 Booth, *Reign of Grace*, 234.
90 Booth, *Reign of Grace*, 246.
91 Booth, *Reign of Grace*, 252–253.
92 *Death of Legal Hope* (*Works*, 1:338, 340).
93 Booth, *Reign of Grace*, 262–263.

Lord has promised that his people shall never perish, he has not assured them freedom from sin. Backsliders "have severely smarted under his correcting hand." The foundation for the believer's security is that he is in covenant with God and as an adopted child he does not depend on he own obedience or efforts.[94]

The law of God takes its place in the mighty plan as the instrument of teaching the sinner the holiness of God and the evils of sin (Paul's pedagogue, Galatians 3:24). From this recognition, the Holy Spirit leads him to acknowledge the equity of God's sentence. Thus, legal sanction is "happily useful" in showing forth the freeness and power of saving grace.[95]

Martin Luther, with far greater power, argues the utility of the law of God, in showing forth the consistency and righteousness of divine will. He identified the wrath of God as his "strange work," in contrast with his "proper work" of forgiveness and grace.[96] That strange work into which he is forced by human pride "is at the service, not in control of that proper work." The Reformer divorced such pure and holy love from all suggestion of legalism. Its willingness to forgive "at the cost of utter self-sacrifice" delivers men from the worst tyrant of all—the wrath of God when it is separated from his love.[97]

Man, as a reasonable creature, designed to propagate his species and fitted for social life, needed a rule of conduct and limitations placed on his duty, to God and to his fellow-creatures, the author pointed out.[98] This rule was provided in the law which Booth described as follows:

> As in the hand of Christ, it is a friend and guide, pointing out the way in which the Christian should walk, so as to express his gratitude to God for his benefits, and to glorify the Redeemer. It shows him also, how imperfect is his own obedience, and so is a happy means of keeping him humble at the foot of sovereign grace, and entirely dependent on the righteousness of his divine Sponsor.... Thus the law and the gospel are mutually subservient to one another, while both agree to promote the happiness of the redeemed, and the glory of their divine Author.[99]

---

94 Booth, *Reign of Grace*, 271.
95 *Death of Legal Hope* (*Works*, 1:360).
96 Martin Luther, *A Commentary Upon the Epistle of Paul to the Galatians* ([Philadelphia]: Salmon S. Miles, 1837), 141–142.
97 Philip S. Watson, *Let God Be God* (Philadelphia: Muhlenberg Press, 1949), 124.
98 *Death of Legal Hope* (*Works*, 1:420).
99 *Death of Legal Hope* (*Works*, 1:435).

Booth recognized the universal impulse to imagine that obedience to the law will bring reward, hoping that a merciful God will respect one's endeavours, recognize an upright heart, and on this foundation, apply to the sinner the merits of Jesus Christ. However, the only salvation, he argued, lies in dropping pretensions to one's own worthiness and acknowledging Jesus as a substitute. Believers are dead to the law that they might live to God, not commit iniquity freely or sin with impunity.[100]

On the matter of repentance, God connected it with his forgiveness, because of the regard it shows to Christ's expiatory death. In no way does the repentance itself compensate for sin or remove its deserved punishment. It cannot be offered by man as a work of righteousness.[101]

The pardon that God affords is necessarily perfect in its freeness, fullness, and eternal qualities: "That is; it must extend to *all* sin; it must be vouchsafed without *any conditions* to be performed by the sinner; and it must be *absolutely irreversible*."[102] For example, the salvation of Saul, the persecutor, stands, not as a particular instance of sovereign bounty, but as an example of what multitudes would enjoy in the years to follow. Or again, the pardon afforded the thief on the cross reveals that men have no solid foundation of hope except in the blood of Christ, and that the vilest need not despair.[103]

Booth again crossed swords with the Arminian tendency toward licentiousness in the face of forgiveness. He contended that pardon operates instead to "bias your affections on the side of virtue." Sin stands out in all its evil against the purity and will of God.[104]

The doctrine of grace so possessed Booth's heart and mind that he saw it to dominate every other doctrine in his theology. He defined it as, "the eternal and absolutely free favour of God, manifested in the vouchsafement of spiritual and eternal blessings to the guilty and the unworthy."[105] Grace has no connection with works in any degree. It is no respecter of persons, and no one of any rank or character has grounds for application for admission into the kingdom of God. All are on equal footing with regard to access to God and their expectation of relief.[106]

---

100 *Death of Legal Hope* (*Works*, 1:396).
101 *Divine Justice* (*Works*, 3:33).
102 Booth, *Reign of Grace*, 107.
103 Booth, *Reign of Grace*, 117–118, 121–127.
104 Booth, *Reign of Grace*, 143.
105 Booth, *Reign of Grace*, 16–17.
106 Booth, *Reign of Grace*, 23–24.

Booth pointed to the doctrine of Paul and the early disciples which was run through with the same awareness of grace that colours all of his own writings:

> ... grace does not only appear; it shines, reigns, triumphs:

> It is the only thing... All those fine distinctions, invented by the proud philosopher, or the self-righteous moralist, which tend in any degree to support the opinion of human worthiness and to obscure our views of divine grace, are by them entirely set aside, and totally annihilated.[107]

Booth, of course affirmed the doctrine of the resurrection of the dead and understood that the spirit, when separated from the body at death is "lodged in eternal mansions, and abiding at the source of all felicity."[108] The author continues, "glorious is that sublime blessedness which is possessed by the separate spirits of saints in heaven; it, nevertheless, comes short of that happiness which shall be enjoyed in their *whole persons*."[109] This celestial fellowship continues until the resurrection and judgement. When the body, itself, is raised, it will possess its personal identity, but will be of such a different quality as to fit it for its reunion with its immortal spirit.[110]

He followed Paul (1 Corinthians 15), in the main idea, but filled in some details. His emphasis on the bodily resurrection is strong, and there is no suggestion of the Greek concept that the body is merely the prison of the spirit. Moss states this important truth:

> Unless the body were destined to rise again, the spirit, though immortal, would still be separated from the body; man would still be rent asunder. But the Resurrection of our Lord brings to us the good news that what is rent asunder by death is to be joined together again; it is as complete persons, not as disembodied spirits, that we are to be united with God in Heaven.[111]

As a surmise on what lies beyond, Booth ventured the thought that

---

107 Booth, *Reign of Grace*, ix.
108 Booth, *Reign of Grace*, 312.
109 Booth, *Reign of Grace*, 319.
110 Booth, *Reign of Grace*, 320–322.
111 C.B. Moss, *The Christian Faith* (London: Society for Promoting Christian Knowledge, 1943), 121.

man's capacities for heavenly enjoyment will increase, "For the Deity is an infinite source of blessedness; and finite vessels may be forever expanding, and forever filling, in that ocean of All-sufficiency...this is the end of the victorious reign of grace."[112]

---

112 Booth, *Reign of Grace*, 326–327.

William Kiffin

An important seventeenth-century London Baptist pastor and theologian, who did much to develop the argument for closed communion that Booth later defended

6

COMMUNION AND BAPTISM

The relation of believer's baptism to the Lord's Supper raised an issue on which Baptists were divided in the time of Booth. They are still divided on it. An early record of the controversy goes back to the protest made by William Kiffin, Baptist preacher, merchant, and Commonwealth M.P., who attacked John Bunyan for sitting at the Lord's Table with Paedobaptists.[1] As late as 1742, Mr. Baskerville, a member of one of the London Baptist churches, was expelled for communing occasionally in the state churches, a disciplinary action approved by all of the London churches.[2]

OPEN AND CLOSED COMMUNION

Two of Booth's contemporaries, Daniel Turner of Abingdon and John Ryland of Northampton, advocated open communion under the assumed names of "Pacificus" and "Candidus," insisting on forbearance in such "non-essential" matters.[3] Turner thought the Lord's table should be open to all "who appear to love the Lord Jesus Christ in sincerity… a standing, visible, external pledge and means, of that divine union and fellowship all true Christians have with Christ and one another in one

---

1   E.A. Payne, *The Fellowship of Believers, Baptist Thought and Practice Yesterday and Today.* (London: Kingsgate Press, 1944), 55.

2   Richard B. Cook, *The Story of the Baptists in All Ages and Countries* (Baltimore: R.H. Woodward and Company, 1889), 179.

3   "Memoir of the Author" (*Works*, 1:xlii).

body, as morally distinguished and separated from the world."[4] With this principle of the open table, neither Abraham Booth nor Andrew Fuller could agree,[5] but Robert Hall, an equally influential Baptist leader, supported it.[6] In most matters, Booth was a High Calvinist, but in his views on communion, he resembled Zwingli.[7]

It is erroneous to attribute either to all Baptists or to Zwingli, the view that the Lord's supper is only a token and "memorial" of the Lord's passion and death.[8] Referring to Zwingli's *Confession* to King Francis, Dr. Wheeler Robinson shows that even the Swiss Reformer acknowledged the spiritual presence of Christ at his supper to be realized by the believer.[9] In this he resembles the present day statement of the British Baptists that the supper is a "special means of grace, but not, be it noted, a means of special grace."[10] Christ is really present at the supper, as he is present in the preaching of the Word, in prayer, and in other means of worship.

A Baptist minister friend of Booth had been called to the pastoral office of a London church which observed mixed communion. Having some reservations in his own mind relative to the propriety of the practice, he went to Booth for counsel. The visit resulted in a series of letters in which Booth stated his position and arguments on the communion question.

These letters were the basis of his work published in 1778, entitled *An Apology for the Baptists*, with the subtitle, "in which they are vindicated from the imputation of laying an unwarrantable Stress on the Ordinance of Baptism; and against the Charge of Bigotry, in refusing Communion at the Lord's Table to Paedobaptists." The object of the work was to oppose the principle of mixed communion.[11] Booth sets forth his stand:

> The point controverted between us and our Paedobaptist brethren, is not whether unbaptized believers may, according to the laws of Christ,

4 Payne, *Fellowship*, 55.
5 Joseph Ivimey, *A History of the English Baptist* (London: Isaac Taylor Hinton, 1830), 4:124, note.
6 A.C. Underwood, *A History of the English Baptists* (London: Kingsgate Press, 1947), 182.
7 Payne, *Fellowship*, 55.
8 *The Lord's Supper: A Baptist Statement* (London: The Carey Kingsgate Press, Ltd., 1951), 19.
9 H. Wheeler Robinson, *The Life and Faith of the Baptists* (London: Methuen and Company, Ltd., 1927), 118, note.
10 *Lord's Supper*, 20.
11 "Memoir of the Author" (*Works*, 1:xlii).

be admitted to communion; for here we have no dispute; but, *What is baptism*, and *who* are the proper subjects of it? ... They, in general, admit, that *immersion* in the name of the triune God, on a profession of faith in Jesus Christ, is *baptism, real baptism*; while our fixed and avowed persuasion will not permit us to allow, that *infant sprinkling*, though performed with the greatest solemnity, is worthy of the name. Consequently, though they, consistently with their own principles may receive *us* to communion among *them*, yet we cannot admit them to fellowship with us at the Lord's table, without contradicting our professed sentiments. For it appears to us, on the most deliberate inquiry, that immersion is not a *mere circumstance* or a *mode* of baptism, but *essential* to the ordinance: so that, in our judgment, he who is not immersed is not baptized.[12]

Is it not possible, however, Booth inquired, to attain peace and harmony without having to condone infant sprinkling as divine ordinance, in direct opposition to the Baptist conviction?[13] He could not see that the Lord's supper was intended as a test of brotherly love among Christians, contending that sitting down at the holy supper should be considered as "*the criterion* of my love to individuals, or to any Christian community does not appear from the word of God." The Father had a greater purpose in establishing it as a memorial of his love for his children and Christ's death for them. Those two great facts are to be the subject of contemplation at the Lord's table.[14]

Free communion, Booth reasoned, eventuated in a "tendency to exclude baptism from the worship of God."[15] If it is permissible for one believer to participate simply as a believer, without baptism, then it is only just to offer the table to anyone who desires it.[16]

The author distinguished between receiving Paedobaptists into communion, which would be "openly to connive at an error," and inviting their ministers into Baptist pulpits. In the latter instance he contended, it is not necessary to overrule any command of God or place approval on man-made accessories to worship. These ministers are invited in the expectation that they will preach the gospel which

12 *Vindication of the Baptists from the Charge of Bigotry, in Refusing Communion at the Lord's Table to Paedobaptists* [*The Baptist Library: A Republication of Standard Baptist Works*, eds. Charles G. Sommers, William R. Williams, and Levi L. Hill (New York: Lewis Colby & Co., 1846), 1:45].

13 *Vindication of the Baptists* (*Baptist Library*, 1:63).

14 *Vindication of the Baptists* (*Baptist Library*, 1:45–46).

15 *Vindication of the Baptists* (*Baptist Library*, 1:53).

16 *Vindication of the Baptists* (*Baptist Library*, 1:49).

Baptists and Paedobaptists hold in unison.[17]

It would appear from the foregoing statement that Booth had only a limited idea of the Lord's supper as an instrument of proclaiming the gospel, as efficacious as preaching. A.J.B. Higgins refers to the supper as a "proclamation" and remembrance,[18] an interpretation with which Booth would agree. Booth does not accept as a logical consequence, however, the necessity for letting the supper preach to whoever it will, and he does not account for this aspect in his references to the preaching of Paedobaptists in Baptist churches.

The differences in communion practice, noted in Chapter 1, still continue in British Baptist churches. A few continue the tradition of permitting non-members to remain for the observance of the Lord's supper as their answer to 1 Corinthians 11:26, "As often as ye eat this bread and drink the cup, ye proclaim the Lord's death till he come." Strict Baptist churches, which included the Little Prescott Street Church in the eighteenth century, maintain a "closed table," to which only baptized believers are invited. The proclaiming power of the ordinance is thereby restricted to the assembled group of baptized believers. Still other churches open the table "to all believers in Christ."[19]

At the close of his *Apology*, Booth answers a critic, Dr. Mayo:

> According to this gentleman, then, we are *watery bigots*. Well, it does not greatly distress *me* to be thus represented by a sneering antagonist, because I really believe that *much water* is necessary to baptism and am no less confident, that baptism is necessary to communion at the Lord's table.[20]

Booth did allow some variation. In a letter to Orlando Buckley, in 1785, he said he would not think it unlawful for a baptized person occasionally to commune with a Paedobaptist church, but he would inform the presiding minister that neither he nor his people regard it as identifying infant sprinkling with Christian baptism. He added the recommendation that it is worthwhile to travel over twenty miles a few times a year to hold communion with the baptized.[21]

A reviewer of *Apology for the Baptists*, speaks of the eminence of the

---

17   *Vindication of the Baptists* (*Baptist Library*, 1:66).
18   A.J.B. Higgins, *The Lord's Supper in the New Testament* (London: The S.C.M. Press, 1952), 53.
19   *Lord's Supper*, 11.
20   *Apology for the Baptists* (*Works*, 2:505).
21   "Calendar of Letters, 1742–1831", *The Baptist Quarterly*, 6 (1932–1933):175.

writer and proceeds to state his conviction that if Booth had written nothing more, the reviewed work "might well excite the observation of the religious world." His diversity of arguments on the side of strict communion are so "pointed, and strong, that a free communionist may find it no easy task to answer him."[22]

Such seemed to be the case, because no immediate reply to the *Apology* was forthcoming, and Booth seemed to have closed the controversy for a time.[23] The work was widely circulated in England and America and has gone through four editions. It is just possible that Paedobaptists did not judge the work worthy of reply, but in the light of Booth's standing in his denomination and the replies his other works provoked, it can only be said no antagonist felt moved to engage him on this particular ground at this particular time. It may attest to the force of Booth's argumentation that Paedobaptists are no longer offering classic New Testament texts as direct proof for their stand.

The joining of the General and Particular Baptists in the Baptist Union of Great Britain and Ireland in 1892, went far in moderating Booth's strict position among the members of his own denomination. The Baptist claim is that the "Supper remains the Supper of the Lord," and except in instances of Strict Communion sentiment, British Baptists admit fellow believers on the basis of "oneness of membership in Christ."[24] The claim that it is the Lord's table is used by the Strict Communionists as well, however, in their insistence upon the observance of New Testament practice as they see it.

BAPTISM

In 1784, Booth entered the baptismal controversy, publishing a work entitled, *Paedobaptism Examined, on Principles, Concessions, and Reasonings of the most learned Paedobaptists*. In the preface, he said that he had observed for a number of years, how many of the most learned Paedobaptists, when discussing theological subjects, "frequently argue on such principles, admit of such facts, interpret various texts of Scripture in such a manner and make such concessions as are greatly in favour of the Baptists." For his own use, Booth made up a collection

---

22 *The Evangelical Magazine*, 21 (1813):460–1.
23 Ivimey, *History*, 4:36.
24 *Lord's Supper*, 27, 31.

of these references against infant sprinkling and arranged them under different heads of the Paedobaptist controversy. After a considerable amount of work was done on this compilation, a posthumous work of Matthew Henry on infant baptism, edited by Mr. Robins of Daventry, was published. Upon reading this work, Booth determined to answer it.[25] He added extensively to his file of memoranda from Paedobaptist writers and prepared from these materials a work that was destined to be used as a source book on baptism for over 100 years.

Each chapter of *Paedobaptism Examined* opens with a collection of quotations from such outstanding Paedobaptist writers of all ages as Dr. Doddridge, Bishop Taylor, Jonathan Edwards, Stapferus, Vitringa, Hoornbeekius, and Bishop Hoadley, to name but a few, to support his positions on the various topics he pursues. Then follow a series of Booth's own reflections, pointed conclusions favourable to the Baptist position on baptism and drawn from the preceding statements, all replete with additional reinforcing quotations.

Baptism is considered in exhaustive detail from the standpoints of: a positive institution; the significance of the term; its design; the practices of John the Baptist, the Apostles, and the church in succeeding ages, including Greek and Oriental churches; pouring and sprinkling, the design more fully expressed by immersion; no express precept or precedent in the New Testament for Paedobaptism; the origin of Paedobaptism, the utility of baptism; old and modern grounds for Paedobaptism; and infant communion. The summary illustrates and confirms Booth's main argument that immersion of professing believers is New Testament baptism.[26]

Throughout the intricacies of his study, Booth returned to Chillingsworth's statement, "the Bible is the religion of the Protestants," as his incontestable stand.[27] He explained:

Baptism being a gracious appointment of God, it must have an important meaning; and as it is a positive ordinance, the whole of its design must be fixed by divine institutions for we have no more authority to invent a signification for any rite of holy worship than we have to appoint the rite itself. The design of baptism, therefore, must be learned from the New

---

25   Abraham Booth, *Paedobaptism Examined, on the Principles, Concessions, and Reasonings of the Most Learned Paedobaptists* (London: Ebenezer Palmer, 1829), 1:iv ff.

26   Booth, *Paedobaptism Examined*, Vols. 1–2.

27   Booth, *Paedobaptism Examined*, 1:20, 314.

Testament, and from such parts of that sacred volume as have an immediate reference to it.[28]

Dr. John Clifford, at the Baptist World Congress of 1911, affirmed that: "The deepest impulse of Baptist life has been upholding the sole and exclusive authority of Jesus Christ against all possible encroachment."[29] To this, Pierre Charles Marcel, in his masterful study of the Reformed belief, declares, "We regard Holy Scripture as a whole," and proceeds to develop scripturally the concept of baptism as the need of the Covenant of Grace, necessarily including the children of believers. He condemns the dependence upon New Testament texts, which Karl Barth employs in his new position, as cutting the Bible in two, causing a wide chasm between the Old and New Testament. He sees an essential oneness in the sacraments of the Old and New Testaments, in their significance, content, the nature of their efficacy, and their religious and moral demands.[30]

Booth finds almost unanimous agreement among his authors on the intention of baptism as representing, "the *death*, *burial*, and *resurrection* of Christ; the *communion* his people have with him in those momentous facts; and their interest in the blessing thence resulting."[31] It follows, he reasoned, that if baptism is to serve as a perfect picture of cleansing from sin, immersion is the only mode that represents a total washing.[32]

His further investigations indicated to him that the practice of immersion preceded sprinkling or pouring and prevailed in England until the reign of James I. John Calvin was largely responsible for the change that then followed, coupled with a growing spirit of false modesty and "nicety" in the society of the day. "Calvin's form of administering the sacraments," Booth observed, "was probably the first in the world, that prescribed pouring absolutely."[33]

The New Testament passages usually referred to in support of infant baptism, he concluded, could only prove that it is permitted or not forbidden, since all instances where baptism is commanded pertain to adults. Paedobaptism, therefore, depends entirely on analogy

---

28 Booth, *Paedobaptism Examined*, 1:159.
29 Payne, *Fellowship*, 17.
30 P.C. Marcel, *The Biblical Doctrine of Infant Baptism, Sacrament of the Covenant of Grace* (London: James Clarke & Co. Ltd., 1953), 23, 16.
31 Booth, *Paedobaptism Examined*, 1:160.
32 Booth, *Paedobaptism Examined*, 1:162.
33 Booth, *Paedobaptism Examined*, 1:249, 262.

and inference.[34]

Marcel, Cullman, and Flemington[35] agree with the recent criticism of Barth,[36] that the Paedobaptist position cannot be defended on the basis of direct Scripture, but they contend for the authenticity of indirect evidence and analogy: "In theology, that which follows by legitimate deductions from scriptural norms is as exact as that which is explicitly stated."[37] On these very grounds they attack the Baptists for their insistence on believer's baptism for believers' children, when no such necessity is cited in Scripture.[38] It is pertinent here to note the statement of Dr. Payne, in reply to T. W. Manson's *Baptism in the Church*:

> The abandonment of the quest for scriptural or apostolic authority in regard to those who should be the subjects of baptism surely raises much wider and more serious issues than the immediate question before us...It opens the door to many other departures from apostolic practice.[39]

From a morass of quotation and argumentation, we lift Booth's simple statement of the Baptist position:

> When we oppose the baptism of infants, it is not because of their tender age; but because they neither do nor can profess faith in the Son of God. Whenever we meet with such as are denominated by the apostle...believing children, [Titus 1:6] whoever may be their parents, or whatever may be their age, we have no objection to baptize them. A credible profession of repentance and faith being all we desire, in reference to this affair, either of old or young.[40]

The author lamented that paedobaptism "is calculated to do immense mischief to the souls of men," by misleading the recipient into believing he has received the new birth, been cleansed from sin and become a child of God, by an act performed before he was even aware. Quoting his favourite author, John Owen, he agrees that, "the father of lies himself could not easily have invented a more deadly poison for the

---

34 Booth, *Paedobaptism Examined*, 1:309.

35 W. F. Flemington, *The New Testament Doctrine of Baptism* (London: S. P.C. K., 1948), 131.

36 Karl Barth, *The Teaching of the Church Regarding Baptism* (London: S.C.M. Press, 1948), 42–4.

37 Marcel, *Infant Baptism*, 189–190.

38 Oscar Cullmann, *Baptism in the New Testament.* (London: S.C.M. Press, Ltd., 1950), 26.

39 E.A. Payne, "Professor T. W. Manson on Baptism," *Scottish Journal of Theology* 3 (1950):39.

40 Booth, *Paedobaptism Examined*, 1:367.

souls of sinners; as they are taught, by those unscriptural dogmas, to rest satisfied with a supposed regeneration by their baptism."[41] This statement resembles the Baptist position that has been cited regarding infant baptism:

It bolsters up the erroneous notion that infants are guilty at birth and are in peril if they die unbaptized. It fosters the superstitious idea that a Christian sacrament can have any meaning or offset apart from the faith of the recipient. It obscures the truth that salvation is by faith alone, independent of all priestly ministrations and all ecclesiastical rites. It is incompatible with the spiritual principles of the Protestant Reformation, and its retention leaves the work of the Reformation incomplete. When, therefore, Baptists persist in their testimony against infant baptism they are not testifying against an isolated and relatively unimportant custom; they are testifying against the whole complex of ideas of which it was a symbol, out of which grow the conception of the Church as primarily a great sacramental Institution, administered by a body of officials vested with spiritual powers in which ordinary Christians could not share.[42]

To such objections, Marcel replies in his restatement of Calvinistic doctrine:

The foundation of baptism is not the supposition that each one is regenerated, nor even regeneration itself, but simply the covenant of God. No more is it a question of proving that the elect are always regenerated by the Holy Spirit in their infancy, before baptism or even before birth. God is free in the distribution of His blessings and can cause the fruit of baptism, as a sign and seal of the promises of the covenant, to be received also at a very advanced age, whether baptism has been administered in adulthood or in infancy.[43]

It is awkward, Booth insists, that "Christ expressed a condescending regard for little children *without* baptizing them, or saying a word about it; therefore we should manifest an affectionate care for infants *by* baptizing them!"[44] The apostles surely knew their Master's position on this and sought to follow his teaching. Their practice and writings

---

41 Booth, *Paedobaptism Examined*, 1:443.
42 Bryan, F.C. and R.L. Child, *Concerning Believer's Baptism* (London: The Kingsgate Press, 1943), 59–60.
43 Marcel, *Infant Baptism*, 233.
44 Booth, *Paedobaptism Examined*, 2:161.

should be reliable guides to his will in the matter, but Booth found no justification for Paedobaptism in the commands of Christ or the practice of his disciples.[45]

Again we turn to Marcel for the Paedobaptist answer: "Had our Lord wished the reception of children into this ever valid covenant to be discontinued He would have said so in order that no one might be in any doubt."[46]

Booth comments on the occasional Baptist practice of dedicating children, when specifically requested by the parents. The usual service included a Scripture reading, an exhortation to the parents concerning the child's education, a prayer of gratitude to God for his gift of the child, closing with an earnest recommendation of the child to his Maker. In such he saw no positive rite.[47]

In the twentieth century Karl Barth reopened the baptismal controversy with his move onto the side of believer's baptism, based on faith.[48] Cullmann, who refers to Barth's study as "the most serious challenge to Infant Baptism which has over been offered," holds, however, that "it belongs to the essence of this general Baptism effected by Jesus, that it is offered in entire Independence of the decision of faith and understanding of those who benefit from it."[49]

Flemington seeks to answer the problem of faith in infant baptism by shifting the responsibility for it to "the worshipping Church and Christian parents." He suggests that those who insist on the necessity of faith for any objective efficacy in infant baptism may be betraying their own "lack of faith concerning the method of divine revelation and the power of God to fulfill his own promises."[50]

Emil Brunner lends his substantial support to believer's baptism, on the other hand, declaring that, "Where one separates the Word of God and faith to this extent, the character of the *sacrament* is invalidated; then ineluctably the proposition of the Reformation holds: *Nullum sacramentum sine fide.*"[51] In this position, he is joined by H.G. Marsh[52]

---

45 Booth, *Paedobaptism Examined*, 2:134.

46 Marcel, *Infant Baptism*, 191.

47 Booth, *Paedobaptism Examined*, 2:163.

48 Barth, *Teaching*, 43.

49 Cullmann, *Baptism*, 7–8, 20.

50 Flemington, *Doctrine of Baptism*, 144, 136.

51 Emil Brunner, *The Divine-Human Encounter* (London: S.C.M. Press, 1944), 131.

52 H.G. Marsh, *The Origin and Significance of the New Testament Baptism* (Manchester: Manchester University Press, 1941), 202–203.

and by Dr. Payne, who points out, "It is surely entirely arbitrary and unsatisfactory, when setting out the main ideas connected with New Testament baptism, to omit penitence and faith."[53]

Booth questioned the reason for Protestant Paedobaptists in general laying so much emphasis on proselyte baptism, Jewish circumcision, and ecclesiastical tradition, in favour of infant baptism. He concluded that they must draw upon ancient custom or tradition in proof of their point since the New Testament does not provide a divine command.[54] "Few mistakes in theology have, indeed," he states, "either so extensive or so pernicious an Influence upon the church and worship of the New Testament, as those which tend to confound the Christian church with the Jewish synagogue."[55]

Barth speaks out strongly on this question:

Circumcision refers to natural birth; it is the sign of the election of the holy lineage of Israel, which with the birth of the Messiah achieved its goal, so that therewith this sign lost its meaning. The succession of those who believed this promise and in this faith were true children of Abraham, was, however, already in pre-messianic Israel (according to Romans 4) in no way identical with the succession of the race and the circumcision of its (male!) members. And so properly, the succession of those called to the Church of the new covenant (according to John 1:12f.) is plainly not dependent on a racial succession, not on family or nation, but come in this way: in the life of the individuals now here in this manner, now there in another, there comes an acceptance... of Jesus, a faith in His name. It is this which gives him the power to become a child of God.[56]

Although John's baptism was, without doubt, a rite of incorporation into Israel, "prepared to meet her God," E.A. Payne insists it was "a rite to which the essential preliminary, in John's mind, was repentance and the confession of sin."[57]

Cullmann on the other hand, states that "Christian Baptism takes over at the same time the function of proselyte baptism and circumcision."[58] Marcel, who follows him, bases his entire case for infant

---

53   Payne, "Professor T. W. Manson on Baptism," 53.
54   Booth, *Paedobaptism Examined*, 2:243.
55   Booth, *Paedobaptism Examined*, 2:92.
56   Barth, *Teaching*, 43–44.
57   Payne, "Professor T. W. Manson on Baptism," 52.
58   Cullmann, *Baptism*, 64.

baptism on the covenant of grace with baptism replacing circumcision as the sacrament of admission. He contends that circumcision is robbed of its true nature when judged as a carnal institution.[59]

Portions of a lengthy summary and conclusion will illustrate Booth's manner of argumentation:

> They have admitted the facts on which we reason:...Do we maintain that immersion was the apostolic practice, and that except in extraordinary cases, it was the general custom for thirteen hundred years? They confirm our sentiment,—Do we affirm, that immersion is the present practice of the Greek and Oriental churches, and that those churches include one half of the Christian world? Their own pens bear testimony for us... Do we assert, that the first instance of pouring or sprinkling, instead of immersion, which is expressly recorded, was about the middle of the third century, and then condemned; that the apostate church of Rome... brought pouring into common practice, and that Protestant churches received it from her polluted hands? These being stubborn facts are all acknowledged.—Do we maintain that, in ordinary cases immersion is not prejudicial to health? Paedobaptist physicians without a fee, and medical practice without hesitation, confirm our opinion.—Do we assert, that no power on earth has authority to alter the law of Christ, or to depart from apostolic example in regard to immersion? So do they, in effect, when disputing with Papists, concerning the shared supper.—Is it our opinion, that the extravagant notions of the fathers, in the second and in the beginning of the third century, concerning the great utility of baptism, and their misunderstanding of John iii.5, laid the foundation of Paedobaptism? It is allowed...Do we maintain, that infant baptism and infant communion were Introduced about the same time; that they were supported by kindred arguments; that they were equally common for a course of ages; and that they are still united in the practice of half the Christian world? We have the happiness to find, that these facts are all confirmed by their learned pens.[60]

Booth notes that the Baptists are "honoured with having some of them [Paedobaptists] for our associates in everything except the conclusion."[61]

The performance of this remarkable work was highly pleasing to Baptists, as the *Memoir* attests, stating that the subject was probably

---

59 Marcel, *Infant Baptism*, 151, 155, 158.
60 Booth, *Paedobaptism Explained*, 2:291.
61 Booth, *Paedobaptism Explained*, 2:292.

never "handled in a more masterly manner by any writer in any age or language by the expedient of turning his opponents' own weapons against themselves."[62]

Joseph Ivimey adjudged, "The Baptists confidently leave their cause, so far as human writings are concerned, to the reasonings and arguments of what they consider this unanswered and unanswerable work."[63]

The work was so popular that a second edition was necessary in 1787. This one Booth considerably enlarged, expanding it into two volumes which "exhausted the controversy on the Baptist side of the question."[64]

Edward Williams of Oswestry furnished a two-volume reply for the Paedobaptists. Booth did not consider an answer necessary until a circumstance arose which prompted him, in 1792, to publish *A Defense of Paedobaptism Examined*.[65] In his preface, Booth said he was informed by a letter from a trustworthy source that Williams was spreading a story that Booth confessed Williams' work unanswerable and would declare for infant baptism were it not for the disadvantages attending an open declaration of his sentiments. Booth replied vehemently, dissecting *AntiPaedobaptism Examined* tirelessly, reiterating with another overwhelming array of quotations the issues of his original work. Both authors were unsparing of each other in delicate and indelicate, sarcasm and irony. Booth expressed his opinions on both infant sprinkling and on Williams typically in the following:

When I peruse his Discourse on the Christian's reasons for Glorying in the Cross of Christ, I approve, I am pleased, I am edified; but, when reading his Improvement of Christian Baptism, and particularly of Infant Baptism, I am both disgusted and grieved. In the former, our *crucified* Lord is exalted and presented to view, as the only medium by which the blessings of grace are communicated to perishing sinners. In the latter, baptism, under the Jewish notion of a *ceremonial purification* is represented as producing a wonderful change in the relative state of a sinner, and as the means of obtaining an important variety of spiritual blessings. Yes, to adopt his own very singular terms, that *ceremonial purification* which is operated by a priest, when tinging his fingers, or intinging *even his hand* to put the subject into a *state of* wetness or to effect *a* contaction *between the person and the*

---

62 "Memoir of the Author" (*Works*, 1: xlv).
63 Ivimey, *History*, 4:38.
64 "Memoir of the Author" (*Works*, 1:xlvi).
65 Ivimey, *History*, 4:36.

element is the medium of obtaining immunities, honours, and blessings, in rich variety![66]

In his conclusion, Booth fixed the reader's attention on the peculiarities contained in Williams' work and the grounds of his argumentation, which he satirized thus:

> ... if the Scripture be not decisively express against infant baptism, we are to conclude the apostles practiced it;—that infants have a legal right to the Lord's supper; and that infant communion is merely an impropriety, prudential reasons lying against it;—that the Jews owed their Bible to circumcision;—that baptism ratifies the promises, and authenticates divine revelation;—that baptism gives a legal title to read the Scripture, to all the contents of that sacred volume, and to all the means of conversion;—that the obligation to repentance, to holiness, and to obedience, results from being baptized—that those who were baptized in their infancy, have a stronger and more indubitable title to numerous blessings, than those that were baptized on a personal profession of faith.[67]

Peter Edwards was for some years pastor of the White's Row Baptist Church, Portsmouth Common, but in 1795, he joined the Paedobaptists. He strenuously opposed the Baptists, Booth in particular, in a work entitled *Candid Reasons*.

That same year, James Dore wrote the preface and notes to an anonymous *Reply to Mr. Peter Edwards: The Principles of AntiPaedobaptism, and the Practice of Female Communion Completely Consistent In Answer to the Arguments and Objections of Mr. Peter Edwards in His Candid Reasons: With Animadversions on His Temper and Conduct in that Publication*. The editor, who included this work in the three-volume edition of *Paedobaptism Examined* along with the *Defense of Paedobaptism Examined*, noted:

> Having ascertained, from unquestionable authority, that the following Answer to the *Candid Reasons* of the Rev. Peter Edwards, was written by Mr. Booth, it has been thought proper that it should form a part of these Volumes.[68]

---

66 Booth, *Paedobaptism Explained*, 3:361–362.
67 Booth, *Paedobaptism Explained*, 3:366.
68 Booth, *Paedobaptism Explained*, 3:368.

Dore summarized concisely the distinguishing principles of the Baptists on baptism in his preface, but the ramifications of Booth's and Edwards' argument are too involved to pursue in the limited space afforded here. The following excerpts show the tenor of their writing. Booth quoted repeated references to his character that appeared throughout Edwards' work:

> *Mr. Booth's abilities* are very small ... Mr. B.'s *talent* is quotation and therefore he must quote ... *He is* grossly ignorant ... It seems a marvelous thing, that Mr. B. should be so well acquainted with Thales, and his biographer Diogenes, and at the same time excessively ignorant *of his own Bible* ... He is a scandal to all consistency ... *He is* extremely ridiculous ... *Mr. Booth has a Talmud of his own* ... I think—that his book though written on the Baptist side, *will do* more *towards overturning* the Baptist sentiment than any one that has been written for many centuries ... *Mr. Booth* is artful and crafty ... *He is a* shifter *and a* prevaricator ... *Mr. Booth is very* unfair, *does not speak the truth, has lost his* modesty, *and is guilty of* absolute falsehood ... Finally; Mr. Booth *is one of the* strangest mortals *that ever appeared in the religious world,* and must repent of what he has done.[69]

Booth replied with sarcasm, though not with the venom that Edwards employed against him:

> What a prodigious loss must "the Baptists' side" have sustained, by such a one deserting to the camp of their opposers! The Baptists have, alas! lost a great stock of mental abilities, together with an immense quantity of Latin and logic, of modesty and of candour. Those rare accomplishments might have been employed in defending and adorning their cause, had not that melancholy desertion taken place. Over such a mournful event, they cannot therefore, but greatly lament; and the very *candid reasons* he gives for taking leave of them, are wonderfully adapted to increase their pungent sorrow![70]

The only other Paedobaptist opponent of Booth in this debate was William Miller, who, in his *Catholic Baptism Examined*, pictures Booth as a bee in a garden surrounded by flowers but with only a sting for the Paedobaptists. He acknowledged the need for a work similar to Booth's but charged him with bias, selecting his Paedobaptist quotations to suit his own opinions. Using more than eighty quotations from *Paedobaptism*

---

69 Booth, *Paedobaptism Explained*, 3:421–424.
70 Booth, *Paedobaptism Explained*, 3:460.

Examined, in an attempt to refute Booth's arguments, he admits that Booth's use of 1 Corinthians 7:14 is "with vast force and advantage."[71] Joseph Jenkins entered the controversy in 1805, publishing *A Defense of the Baptists*, primarily against Edwards. In his introduction, Dr. Jenkins stated that Edwards should find satisfaction in the fact that his work was being noticed to the extent that it merited two replies.[72]

Verbose and controversial though they be, Booth's writings on baptism have served far beyond his denominational and geographical circles as classic source-books on the subject.

The baptismal controversy continues today without promise of ready solution. Marcel states the case quite clearly when he says, "these new facts will not change by a single jot the arguments or the method of discussion of those who disagree with us; no more will they afford us a new weapon with which to oppose."[73] There has been a marked improvement in the tone and temper of these debates within the past 150 years. It is to be hoped that the next 150 can bring Baptists and Paedobaptists into happy accord on Scriptural truth.

---

71 William Miller, *Catholic Baptism Examined or Thoughts on the Ground and Extent of Baptismal Administration, &c.* (High-Wycombe, 1793), vi–ix, 13, 156.

72 Joseph Jenkins, *A Defence of the Baptists Against the Aspersions and Misrepresentation of Mr. Peter Edwards, &c.* (Halifax: Jesse Read and Richard Poindexter, 1805), 7–8.

73 Marcel, *Infant Baptism*, 22.

Andrew Fuller

A key English Baptist theologian who was contemporary with Booth and
who believed Booth to be "the first counsellor" of their denomination

7

SUMMARY AND ESTIMATE

The Evangelical Revival had small effect upon London Baptists until late in the eighteenth century.[1] A new era began, however, with the coming to the city of Abraham Booth, John Rippon, and Joseph Ivimey. Their leadership was fresh, vigorous, and spiritual.[2] Booth, without a doubt, was the strongest of them and made the greatest contribution to the revival of the London Baptist work. Dr. W.T. Whitley speaks of "Abraham Booth, without whom nothing was complete for nearly forty years. In thought he was a great champion of Sovereign grace...."[3] He strongly preached the doctrine of election but was in no way hampered in calling upon all to repent and believe on Christ.[4]

Abraham Booth cannot be rated as a figure of first-magnitude, because his name has passed into obscurity outside informed Baptist circles, but a rediscovery of the place of this "steady pioneer"[5] in great movements of thought and action in the eighteenth century, indicates that his unusual talents were invested in eternal matters.

BOOTH THE MAN

The author's impression of Abraham Booth, gained from his portraits, his record of service, his writings, and the observations of his

---

1   A.C. Underwood, *A History of the English Baptists* (London: Kingsgate Press, 1947), 178.
2   Robert G. Torbet, *A History of the Baptists*. (Philadelphia: The Judson Press, 1950), 101.
3   "Leadership and Fellowship", *The Baptist Quarterly*, 6 (1932–1933):371.
4   Underwood, *English Baptists*, 179.
5   W.T. Whitley, *A History of British Baptists* (London: Kingsgate Press, 1932), 259.

contemporaries, is that of a rocklike character, a plain and humble appearance, a solemnity of manner, a consistent Christian conduct, and a keen intellect, sharpened by the drive of sheer will in ceaseless study. That he possessed wit and humour is seen in his writings and recorded observations, particularly in his replies to Edward Williams and Peter Edwards.

Booth's portraits, a miniature in the possession of his son Isaac and an engraving of this by Mackenzie, published in 1807, show him to have a strong face, a fine forehead, steady, serious eyes, an aquiline nose, long chin, and a stern mouth. He did not appear to be a handsome or imposing man, but possessed a dignity and kindliness of bearing, self-possession, and assurance. The engraving shows him considerably older than the miniature, quite evidently broken in health, with a greater appearance of the solemnity which he always attached to his ministerial office. In his *Kingdom of Christ* Booth expressed the sentiment that coloured much of his conduct as a pastor, "Where, upon earth, are we to expect solemnity, if not in the pulpit? There a man should be serious and solemn as death."[6]

Although his writings are warmly devotional and his sermons are filled with evangelistic zeal, Booth seems to have been of a colder, more intellectual nature, perhaps, than Andrew Fuller—their personalities contrasting in somewhat the manner of their physical frames. Booth was spare and muscular, while Fuller was large and fleshy. In small part, the explanation for Fuller's memory surviving Booth's more positively may be the contrast between the temperament of the two men, Fuller's warmth proving more appealing then and now. That both were possessed of evangelistic spirit, sound judgement, and Christian devotion is unquestioned. Fuller, however, went further than Booth in the closure of the gulf between the General and Particular Baptists, which was to come about at the end of the nineteenth century and held the strategic position in the development of the Foreign Mission Society.

It has been much easier to find references to the "venerable" Abraham Booth than critical statements assessing his shortcomings. Aside from the venom exhibited by some few Paedobaptist authors, Booth seems to have been regarded with almost universal respect and love. Andrew Fuller provides some helpful insight into the character of the man which contrasts with the complimentary statements almost

---

6   Abraham Booth, *An Essay on the Kingdom of Christ* (London, 1788), 54.

always accompanying references to Booth. Expressing himself on different religious sects, Fuller said:

> Nowhere does Antinomianism grow more than in London. (There is not a man there who properly lifts up a standard against it. Indeed, they are all disposed to compromise matters with it. It gets into all their churches, committees, &c., &c.). Mr. Booth, though a very good man, yet feels no alarm on that score; I think as highly of the integrity and piety of A. Booth as of almost any man I know; but his prejudices are strong, and when once fixed, almost immovable. He and I are nearer together in sentiment by far than he and many others with whom, nevertheless, he is on terms of close friendship; while his conscience has, within a few months, impelled him to publish a book [*Divine Justice Essential to Divine Character?*] against me! I have no intention to answer it.[7]

Despite occasional references to Booth's rigidity, Fuller complimented him by speaking of his late beloved friend, John Sutcliffe as "second in counsel only to Abraham Booth."[8]

Booth reveals much about his own simplicity and integrity in the dedication he wrote to the members of the Little Prescott Street Church in *Death of Legal Hope*:

> You will do well to remember, that the true honour and the real excellence of a christian church consist, not to the number or affluence of its members, not in any thing which may dazzle the eye or command the respect of superficial observers, but in its cordial adherence to the truths of the gospel and the ordinances of Christ, in their primitive purity; in the exercise of mutual fervent love among its members; and in a holy, heavenly, useful conversation. They constitute the principal glory of a church. In proportion as these abound, the Redeemer is honoured and believers are edified. In proportion as these abate, the glory departs, and the interests of religion decline.[9]

He was faithful in all respects as a pastor, holding the interests of his congregation before his own without exception. "He appeared always willing to give up almost everything to the decision of the church;

---

7   T.E. Fuller, *A Memoir of the Life and Writings of Andrew Fuller* (London: J. Heaton & Son, 1863), 124.

8   Fuller, *Memoir*, 295.

9   Booth, *Works*, 3:331.

the consequence was that the church gave up almost everything to his decision."[10]

His unimpeachable Christian conduct and practice, which made him a beloved leader to many of his congregation, were a source of irritation to others. The Church Minutes record a complaint by Brother and Sister Tuck who "declared themselves uncomfortable under our Pastor's ministry on account of his fixing the standard of real piety too high."[11]

In his *Pastoral Cautions* Booth gave a side-light on his own experience that presents another aspect of the shepherd-flock relationship than is to be found in the flood of eulogies at his death:

> It is not unlikely that, in a course of years, some of your people, who had expressed a warm regard to your ministry, and perhaps considered you as their spiritual father; may become, without any just reason, your violent opposers, asperse your ministerial character, and wish to be rid of you....
>
> Among the dissatisfied, it is probable, some will complain of your ministry being dry, legal, and of an Arminian cast: while others, it may be will quarrel with it under a supposition, that you dwell too much on the doctrines of divine grace and verge toward Antinomianism. My own ministry, however, has been the subject of loud complaint, in these opposite ways, and that at the very same time.[12]

The author has been impressed, that despite these evidences of occasional discord and disagreement where Booth is concerned, he was a man possessed of an unusually admirable and consistent Christian character. He appears to have kept free of over-enthusiasm, at the same time he avoided dry formality. In almost every instance, he showed himself to be reasonable, kind, understanding, possessed of sound common sense, steering a steady middle course through years of denominational awakening. There is nothing vague or uncertain about the character of Abraham Booth, and for all his plainness and humility, he seems to have won the widest regard in his time for his pure Christianity.

There is almost no reference to Booth as a family man beyond the

---

10   Joseph Ivimey, *A History of the English Baptist* (London: Isaac Taylor Hinton, 1830), 4:375.

11   Quoted Ernest F. Kevan, *London's Oldest Baptist Church (Wapping 1633–Walthamstow 1933)* (London: Kingsgate Press, 1933), 129, from Little Prescott Street Church Minutes.

12   Booth, *Works*, 3:173–174.

fact that he was happily married for forty years and had a houseful of children, as mentioned in Chapter 2. In *Pastoral Cautions*, he admonished consideration for the preacher's wife, "To this end, except on extraordinary occasions, when impelled by duty, spend your evenings at home."[13] This, coupled with his repeated cautions against visiting unattached ladies of the congregation unnecessarily, indicate a thoughtfulness for Mrs. Booth and his family.

BOOTH THE BAPTIST SERVANT

There is no question that Booth's pastoral leadership in what was then the strongest Baptist church in the world was strategic. His emphasis on spiritual and moral rectitude was absolutely basic for Christian strength and accomplishment; he established these ideals in his church, and he was able to lead his membership in a strong program of Christian evangelism and service. The organizations of the Little Prescott Street Baptist Church: the Prayer and Alms Society, the Sunday School, the Evening School, and the village evangelistic groups, bear eloquent testimony to the vision and leadership of this great pastor.

While Booth was the pastor, the Little Prescott Street Church produced a number of leaders who served in many different areas of Christian and denominational work. William Fox organized the Sunday School Society which gave form and direction to the movement, causing it to spread through many denominations throughout England and beyond. Joseph Gutteridge and William Taylor, wealthy deacons, had a vision of a Baptist college in London. As seen in Chapter 4, Taylor gave upwards of £5,000 for property and to the Education Society, resulting in the founding of Stepney Academy, which grew into Regent's Park College, Oxford. Ten young men went into the ministry from the church membership during Booth's thirty-seven years as pastor.

Beyond the limits of his own congregation, Booth gave a wise and positive leadership in denominational affairs. He acted in widening the scope of the Baptist Fund, in its aid to new or struggling churches and preachers, in city or country; he was instrumental in reorganizing the Education Society; and supported whole-heartedly the new Baptist Missionary Society. Joseph Ivimey says, "To his exalted usefulness,

---

13   Booth, *Works*, 3:155.

in the formation of holy and benevolent purposes in the minds of his people, the Baptist Fund owes its chief endowments; and the Academical Institution at Stepney, its entire foundation."[14] He it was who "laid down the lines" of the Society for the Encouragement and Support of Itinerant Preaching, existing now as the Home Mission Society under the present Baptist Union.[15] Under Booth's direction, Thomas Sheraton, one of his members and a minister, led a group from Little Prescott Street Church in a special program of preaching the gospel in the villages around London. "Hall and Sutcliffe had made Northamptonshire a focus for propagating the gospel in foreign parts. Booth made London the twin focus for propagating it in England. The Champion of Grace was the Champion of Home Missions."[16]

BOOTH THE AUTHOR

With his writing ministry, Booth reached a far wider area than the London circle. The *Encyclopedia Americana* makes the following summary statements:

> ...His works were immensely popular in Baptist religious circles, and many editions of his most noted works were published. Some of them were translated into the languages of most of the countries of Europe where Baptist propaganda was then being carried on. Even today they are looked upon in England as the most important word on the Baptist question.[17]

Dr. John Westby-Gibson points out that *Death of Legal Hope* and *Reign of Grace* were translated and printed abroad.[18] Research in the National Library of Holland revealed other of his works in translation, as will be noted in Appendix II. Certain other of Booth's works were translated into Welsh. Of the importance of Booth's works, a reviewer in 1814 said:

---

14 Ivimey, *History*, 4:379.

15 *Transactions of the Baptist Historical Society*, 6 (1918):372.

16 W.T. Whitley, *Calvinism and Evangelism in England, Especially in Baptist Circles* (London: Kingsgate Press, 1933), 37.

17 *The Encyclopedia Americana* (New York: 1946), 4:251.

18 John Westby-Gibson, "Booth, Abraham", *Dictionary of National Biography*, 5:373–374.

... From the time he became a christian the remarkably strong lines of his mental and moral character were formed under the prevalent influence of evangelical truth. He could not be frivolous—he gave the world no trifles from the pen or from the press. The volumes before us exhibit a monument of industrious application, of laborious research, and of sharpened intellect, united to exercise and increase the energies of a man of God. In this light they will be regarded as long as the most important subjects shall interest the christian world.[19]

The most enduring of Booth's publications has been *The Reign of Grace*. When it appeared in the collected works of Booth in 1813, the reviewer gave the following judgement:

To say that it is a masterly performance is only repeating the public opinion, long since expressed in Holland as well as in Britain, in a manner not to need our eulogy. It is already in possession of the approbation of the friends of vital godliness of every denomination to an extent rarely attained by modern works of divinity.[20]

This judgement is amply attested in the fact that in the 183 years since it was first published in 1768, it has been printed in forty-two editions, including at least one Dutch translation. *The Reign of Grace* has appeared in more than twenty-five American editions. Regarding the edition in 1949, Peter de Visser, general manager of the William B. Eerdmans Publishing Company says:

We re-published *The Reign of Grace* because it was in keeping with our program of restoring... Calvinistic literature which had been buried or forgotten, but for which we felt there was an underlying demand for study and reference. Our decisions in these matters have been borne out by public acceptance...[21]

The reviews of this edition have been highly laudatory. A consensus of opinion from them is that through the years, it has achieved a reputation as a standard work of grace; that the qualities of this classic reveal why the publishers turned back the pages of church history to satisfy the theological mind; that it is food for the hungry and strong

---

19 "Account of Religious Publications", *The Baptist Magazine*, 6 (1814):164.
20 "Account of Religious Publications", 164.
21 Peter de Visser, Manuscript Letter.

meat to strengthen the weak.

Paedobaptism Examined was Booth's most controversial work. It received the highest acclaim from many and the highest censure from many others. The massive three-volume work, verbose though it certainly is, is a veritable storehouse on the history of baptism and has been used extensively as source-book for other books on baptism. Two British authors, R. Pengilly and R. Ingham, quote Booth's materials on most of the pages of their works. Ingham wrote *A Handbook on Christian Baptism* in 1865, and Pengilly published *The Scripture Guide to Baptism* in 1836. The influence of this work on British Baptist thought was considerable, reinforcing their confidence in what they considered to be the Scriptural teaching on baptism. It is the most exhaustive work on the subject ever published by the denomination.

In America, *Paedobaptism Examined* has been used more as a source than any other work on baptism. Some of the authors have produced smaller works under different titles, using the entire outline verbatim, and almost all of the contents are from Booth's three-volume work. A partial list of American authors using Booth's material extensively are: J. Gilchrist Lawson, Thomas Westlake, Thomas Baldwin, John T. Christian, T.B. Kingsbury, and D.C. Haynes.

One far-reaching result of *Paedobaptism Examined* in connection with its American influence deserves mention. Adoniram Judson left America for India under appointment of the Congregationalists. Kevan says:

> Anticipating that he would have much to do with William Carey, the Baptist, he resolved to study Abraham Booth's work on the voyage. This he did in order that he might know beforehand all that Carey might have to say on baptism and so be ready to defend himself. By the study of Abraham Booth's book, however, he became convinced of the error of infant sprinkling and saw the truth of believer's baptism by immersion.[22]

This is supported, at least in part, by Judson's own words in the preface to the Indian edition of a sermon on Christian baptism. He stated that the publication of the sermon is due to requests from those who had heard it, and that he might furnish a more full and satisfactory statement of the reasons for his change. In Judson's words, "For many of the testimonies,

22   Kevan, *London's Oldest Baptist Church*, 127.

inserted in this discourse, the author acknowledges himself indebted to Mr. Booth's *Paedobaptism Examined*...Calcutta, Nov. 1812."[23] On May 18, 1814, a convention of Baptists from eleven states and the District of Columbia organized, for the support of the Judsons, The General Missionary Convention of the Baptist Denomination in the United States.[24] The following quotation gives further evidence of the influence of Booth's thought among British Baptists:

> The Baptist Fund sends his publications, *On The Kingdom of Christ* and *Pastoral Cautions* in every grant of books made to young ministers. If they would resolve to do this also in regard to his *Paedobaptism Examined* it might lead to its republication. It is not to the credit of the denomination, that a work of so much labour and research should be out of print. It will be an evidence of great laxity, and want of evangelical zeal, when the Baptists overlook and forget the excellence of the works and character of Abraham Booth.[25]

Booth's correspondence with Dr. William Rogers, pastor of the First Baptist Church of Philadelphia, Pennsylvania, indicates a personal touch with America, in addition to American Baptists' extensive use of his published works. Two letters are of greater importance, one on the slavery issue, dated March 7, 1795 and one on a question of baptism being debated in the Philadelphia Baptist Association. An excerpt from the 1791 Minutes reads as follows:

> Dr. Rogers read a paragraph of a letter from the Rev. Abraham Booth of London, directed to himself, in which was intimated the expediency of our reconsidering the decision of this Association, in 1788, respecting "the invalidity of Baptism when administered by an unbaptized person." "Agreed to refer it to the next meeting of the Association."[26]

In the Minutes of the following year, there appears a note, which indicates that Booth's suggestions were not always acted upon in the

---

23 Adoniram Judson, *A Sermon on Christian Baptism* (Boston: Bould, Kendall and Lincoln, 1846), ii.

24 *Annual Reports of the American Bible Society* (New York: Reprinted for the Society, 1838), 1:392.

25 Ivimey, *History*, 4:379.

26 *Minutes of the Philadelphia Baptist Association, From A.D. 1707 to A.D. 1807*, ed. A.D. Gillette (Philadelphia: American Baptist Publication Society, 1851), 270–271.

affirmative. That entry reads as follows:

> A query respecting the validity of baptism by an unordained and unbaptized administrator, referred in the sixth section of October 5, in our minutes of last year, was taken up, and determined in the negative.[27]

Most of the published works of Abraham Booth appeared in American editions, numbering more than fifty of his various works altogether. Perhaps the best indication of the value placed on his writings in America is seen in the strong endorsement by the Philadelphia Baptist Association and in the use made of them by the American Baptist Publication Society. From the Minutes of the former, we read:

> This Association, receiving information from Dr. Manning, that Mr. Dobson, printer in this city, has now published Mr. Booth's *Apology for the Baptists* and likewise proposes to publish Booth's *Paedobaptism Examined*... do recommend both these pieces as worthy of the perusal of all enquirers after truth, as affording the most convincing and demonstrable evidence in favor of the principles and practice of our churches. As such we recommend them to all our churches and sister Associations.[28]

The 1840 report of the American Baptist Publication Society indicates that the organization published during 1839 "three Tracts and three bound volumes." The report explains that, "The volume enterprise was begun by the issue of [1839] Booth's *Reign of Grace*... The information thus diffused was admirably adapted to the wants of the denomination, and the very best of its kind in each department."[29] The Society published new editions of the same work in 1847 and 1850. In a section in which colportage and evangelism are discussed, is seen, "The teachings of Bunyan and Fuller... [and] Booth... with many more, are powerful helps in the work of cultivating the moral wastes of our country."[30]

Reference was made in Chapter 3 to the A.M. degree which Brown University, in America, conferred upon Booth in 1774. His silence on the matter may be explained by his deep humility and the fact that similar

---

27 *Minutes of the Philadelphia Baptist Association*, 282.

28 *Minutes of the Philadelphia Baptist Association*, 238.

29 J. Newton Brown, *History of the American Baptist Publication Society, from its Origin in 1824 to its Thirty-second Anniversary in 1856* (Philadelphia: American Baptist Publication Society, 1856), 106.

30 Brown, *History*, 261.

degrees were bestowed on Ryland, Beddome, Gill, Fuller, Newman, Carey, and Wallin, to name but some of Booth's contemporaries.[31]

BOOTH THE THEOLOGIAN

From the viewpoint of present-day criticism, Booth's theology appears somewhat rigid, undeveloped, and unoriginal in its approach. He studied hard and seriously the works of British and Continental writers but contributed little that was new or striking. He followed Calvin quite consistently except in regard to the sacraments, in which he would be classified as Zwinglian, if Zwingli can be exactly classified. It is characteristic of the Baptist view that neither system:

> …can claim to be the dominant tradition, and it is interesting to discover that it has frequently been among the Particular Baptists, that is, those Calvinistic in their attitude to questions of election, that Zwinglian views of the Lord's Supper have been most trenchantly advocated.[32]

Marcel calls into question this paradox and declares that bodies which "lay claim to Calvinist doctrine" and differ only on the question of baptism, have wandered far afield in other aspects of their Calvinism.[33]

The names of Andrew Fuller and Robert Hall have lived on with more lustre than that of Abraham Booth, as the moderators of Baptist hyper-Calvinism. This fact, however, cannot alter the evidence, discovered in this research, of Booth's contribution to the transition through his writings and evangelical practices. Both Booth and Fuller, with their mutual interest in the foreign and home mission movements, illustrated the new emphasis on "deed rather than creed." Whitley explains that the circulars of the Northamptonshire Missionary Association:

> …were never digested into one Body of Divinity, and though Fuller and Booth wrote much and deeply, their practical efforts to spread the gospel,

---

31 *Historical Catalogue of Brown University, Providence, R. I., 1764–1894* (Providence, R. I.: P. S. Remington & Co., 1895), 331.

32 E.A. Payne, *The Fellowship of Believers, Baptist Thought and Practice Yesterday and Today* (London: Kingsgate Press, 1944), 51–52.

33 P.C. Marcel, *The Biblical Doctrine of Infant Baptism, Sacrament of the Covenant of Grace* (London: James Clarke & Co. Ltd., 1953), 250–251.

and to educate men who should state it more clearly, did not leave them time to elaborate one general Dogmatic Theology.[34]

A consideration of the early difficulties he had to overcome in educating himself while carrying on secular employment, providing for a large family, creating his own advantages, the later demands of his pastorate, his influential role in all of the work of his denomination, and the multiplicity of his interests—all serve to explain why Abraham Booth did not devote himself to a fully systematized theology. He had little opportunity for one thing and his intensely practical nature, which made all of his study and activity serve him directly in his pastoral and denominational work, would indicate that he had no inclination towards speculative matters for their own sake.

Perhaps the highest tribute that can be paid to Booth, from the standpoint of his writings, is that he was the theologian of the common man. He did not carry his studies to the point of becoming the scholar's theologian, but he went far in presenting Baptist doctrine to his own people in Britain, the United States, and to a limited extent in Europe. He shared the thoughts of greater thinkers with those who would otherwise have been uneducated on the eternal themes with which he dealt. Although his language and some of his concepts possessed many of the crudities and short-comings to be found in eighteenth-century writing, he did exert a safe and sane leadership theologically, moderating rather than stirring up and leading to schism. He was immovable in his convictions, but he was, at the same time, reasonable, his Christian temper fully as evident as his stern insistence and reasoning.

The current movement of Christian thought is away from Humanism and once more toward the concept, caught so arrestingly in Watson's phrase, "Let God be God." Barth brings a difference and a newness to Calvinism, "But it may be claimed that in a real way the Spirit of Calvinism lives again in it and is now reappearing as a quickening force in the thought of man." A number of elements of Calvinism, his view of Scripture, his use of the Old Testament and the basis for Christian ethics, his rigorous doctrine of predestination, disparagement of reason, man's total inability, no longer grip men as they did in Booth's time. The strength of his theology overshadows its weakness, however, and "the insistence on the fact of divine grace as man's sole saving power is already

---

34 Whitley, *Calvinism and Evangelism*, 37.

winning its way as a corrective to loose and ineffectual idealism."[35] The grace of God, the doctrine proclaimed so ably by Abraham Booth, is reigning again in modern theological thought.

CONCLUDING REMARKS

British Baptists have come a long way in the century and a half since the death of Abraham Booth. Much that the old man would discover were he to return, would seem quite alien to him in his exact orthodoxy, with the terms "General" and "Particular" now in disuse since the Union in 1892. "Very few Baptists to-day know what once constituted the difference between Particular and General Baptists. The adjectives have now been dropped."[36] The influence of John Howard Shakespeare, Secretary of the Baptist Union from 1898 to 1925, introduced the new worldwide ecumenical concept to the British Baptists, which, carried to the length which Shakespeare desired, that of reunion with the English Church, would have seemed very strange to Booth. He almost certainly would have joined with John Clifford in the position that represents a large body of Baptist opinion, "unity and differentiation were not inconsistent ideas; and uniformity was, for him both intolerable and deadening."[37]Booth's record of service attests to his belief in cooperative effort within the denomination, and the following statement from his *Confession of Faith*, delivered at the very outset of his Little Prescott Street ministry, gives his concept of inter-denominational fellowship:

> I acknowledge it is my indispensable duty to cultivate a friendly freedom, and brotherly affection, with all those who love our Lord Jesus in sincerity, and bear his image. Such, of whatever denomination they be, I desire to esteem as my brethren, members of the same mystical body, and fellow-heirs of the same eternal inheritance.[38]

It is very doubtful that Abraham Booth, were he living today, would endorse organic union, but the author feels that he would have met the present controversial issue with his accustomed reasonableness, genuine Christian spirit, and abilities as a Christian churchman.

---

35   A. Dakin, *Calvinism* (Philadelphia: The Westminster Press, 1946), 221–222.
36   A.C. Underwood, *A History of the English Baptists* (London: Kingsgate Press, 1947), 216.
37   Underwood, *English Baptists*, 253.
38   "Memoir of the Author" (*Works*, 1:xxxvi).

Booth was outstandingly evangelistic as a London pastor of the eighteenth century and at the same time displayed his awareness of the "social gospel" in his encouragement of the Prayer and Alms Society and his school endeavours within his church, a most progressive move for his day. This blending of faith and works impress the author as a substantial pattern to follow in the present day of revolution.

The renewed interest in Calvinistic writings indicated by the Eerdmans' statement in the preceding section, the acknowledged need for world revival of the scope of England's eighteenth-century Revival, and the proven inadequacies of a purely social and psychological gospel that has failed to grasp the souls of men in the twentieth century, prompt the author to suggest that the emphases of Abraham Booth's life, and his strict but reasonable theology, would stand the test of today's challenges. Controversial preaching and writing, of the eighteenth-century variety, are now outmoded, but the staunchness of Booth's faith and practice, his unimpeachable ethics, and his dogged hard work, it is to be hoped, can never be outdated.

Shortly after Booth's death, a character sketch by William Newman appeared in the memoir attached to Booth's collected works. Some excerpts follow:

As a Christian, he was pre-eminent…

As a Divine, he was a star of the first magnitude. Firm in his attachment to his religious principles, he despised the popular cant about charity, and cultivated genuine candor, which is alike remote from the laxity of latitudinarians and the censoriousness of bigots….

As a Christian Pastor, he shone with distinguished lustre.

As a Literary Man, he was generally acknowledged to belong to the first class among Protestant Dissenters. Without the advantages of a liberal education, he had cut his own way, by the force of a strong, keen mind.

As a universal friend and counsellor, he was exceedingly beloved.[39]

In Newman's own *Memoir*, there appeared additional tribute from a

---

39 "Memoir of the Author" (*Works*, 1:lxxv–lxxx).

man who knew Booth as a spiritual son, "Seldom, indeed, has ever a christian minister been honoured with so considerable a measure of respect and confidence, or possessed such a weight of character, as the Rev. Abraham Booth."[40]

An estimate of Booth's character, appearing in an American publication, *The Baptist Encyclopaedia*, seventy-five years after his death, stated, "Few men have served the cause of God by their writings, sermons, counsels, and example more effectively than Abraham Booth."[41]

This study has been a source of inspiration and rich appreciation to the author, in opening a most significant period in the spiritual history of England and the world, revealing a Christian character as worthy of emulation in the present day, as in his own eighteenth century. The explanations of Booth's personality and contribution that recurred to the author throughout this study, are the workings of the grace of God. Abraham Booth's recognition of this grace came upon him just prior to his change from General to Particular Baptist, with all the force of an original conversion. From the time of that awakening in his own life, his heart, soul, body, and mind were devoted to expressing his indebtedness to his sovereign Lord. Abraham Booth's life might be said to be the strongest argument he ever set forth attesting *The Reign of Grace.*

---

40   George Pritchard, *Memoir of the Rev. William Newman, D.D.* (London: Thomas Ward and Company, 1837), 180.

41   William Cathcart, *The Baptist Encyclopaedia* (Philadelphia: Louis H. Everts, 1881), 114.

COMMERCE IN THE HUMAN SPECIES, AND THE EN-
SLAVING OF INNOCENT PERSONS, INIMICAL TO THE
LAWS OF MOSES AND THE GOSPEL OF CHRIST.

A

S E R M O N,

PREACHED IN

LITTLE PRESCOT STREET, GOODMAN's FIELDS,

JANUARY 29, 1792.

BY ABRAHAM BOOTH.

BEHOLD THE TEARS OF SUCH AS WERE OPPRESSED, AND THEY
HAD NO COMFORTER; AND ON THE SIDE OF THEIR OPPRES-
SORS THERE WAS POWER; BUT THEY HAD NO COMFORTER.
ECCLESIASTES. iv. 1.

REMEMBER HEAVEN HAS AN AVENGING ROD;
TO SMITE THE POOR IS TREASON AGAINST GOD.   COWPER.

L O N D O N:

PRINTED BY L. WAYLAND; AND SOLD BY C. DILLY, POULTRY;
AND T. KNOTT, LOMBARD STREET.

M,DCC,XCII.

APPENDIX I

BOOTH'S MISCELLANEOUS THEOLOGICAL WRITINGS

The demands of his London pastorate, coupled with a concern for the issues of his day, led Booth to preach a variety of sermons and write an assortment of essays on subjects ranging from the slavery question to an opinion on the national establishment of religion, that now compose an interesting portion of his published works. These writings will be considered chronologically, with the funeral addresses grouped under a single heading.

FUNERAL ADDRESSES

As mentioned in connection with his Little Prescott Street pastorate, Abraham Booth was called upon frequently to preach at funerals and interments of his own members, as well as a number of leading Baptists outside his own church.

In 1772, he delivered the sermon, *The Christian Triumph*, at the funeral of Miss Ann Williams, one of his members who had died in her twenty-first year. This message, with the interment address, also by Booth, was subsequently published.

Booth chose as his text, "O death! where is thy sting? O grave! where is thy victory? The sting of death is sin, and the strength of sin is the law; but thanks be to God, which giveth us the victory, through our

Lord Jesus Christ!" (1 Corinthians 15:55–57).[1] In four main points, the preacher dwelt on the evils of death and the grave; the Christian's means of deliverance; his triumph; and his gratitude for the wonderful favour bestowed upon him.

Booth's favourite theme of grace runs through nearly all of his works. In *The Christian Triumph*, he reminded his hearers:

> Yes, my fellow-sinners, if sovereign mercy had not interposed on our behalf, despair had been rational, and damnation certain. But, blessed be God! Grace, divine grace has appeared: it shines in the gospel and reigns through Jesus Christ.[2]

By his own sacrifice and the power of the Holy Spirit, Christ delivers the believer from the "burden" or "love" of sin, and at death his freedom is instantaneous and complete. By overcoming death, the author concludes, Christ makes the grave of no effect, "For what is the grave, but a *repository* for the victims of death?"[3] Booth underlined the fact that God gives the victory—it is not gained by man. The Christian can face death and the grave, not with horror, but "bold as a lion, and firm as a rock. Like some victorious hero, with his foot on the neck of his enemies, he glories over them." Christ, the victor, plucked the sting from death, the author asserted, "and though it pierced his heart and spilt his blood, he exhausted its poison; which has rendered thee [death] utterly incapable of hurting the feeblest of all his followers."[4]

Finally, Booth addressed himself to the young people in the congregation, certainly acquainted with the dead girl and admonished them:

> Young persons are very apt to imagine themselves much wiser, in the things of God, and of greater abilities, than they really are.—Watch against an itch of novelty, both as to doctrines and ministers. For to gratify such an inclination, is the way never to be established in your judgment; never to enjoy solid peace in your minds.—Watch against a dull formality, in the performance of devotional duties; and take heed that you do not make the religious conduct of cold, lifeless professors, whoever they be, a pattern for

---

1   Booth, *Works*, 3:224.
2   Booth, *Works*, 3:227.
3   Booth, *Works*, 3:230–231, 233.
4   Booth, *Works*, 3:235, 237, 238.

your imitation. Watch, then, for ye know not but the time of *your* departure may be at hand.[5]

A series of interment addresses are included in his published works, but their similarity and repetition of sentiments expressed more fully in his Calvinistic works, prompts the writer to forego more than a listing of them: Ann Williams, 1772; Thomas Wilton, 1776; Benjamin Wallin, 1782; Samuel Stennett, 1795; and Joseph Swain, 1795.[6]

The Christian's Happiness in the Heavenly State, the address at the funeral of Mr. S. Gill, preached in 1786, merits more detailed attention. Booth's text was, "They shall hunger no more, neither thirst anymore, neither shall the sun light on them, nor any heat. For the Lamb, which is in the midst of the throne shall feed them, and shall lead them unto living fountains of waters, and God shall wipe away all their tears from their eyes" (Revelation 7:16–17).

Booth spoke first of the sorrow attending the Christian throughout his entire earthly walk. Repentance or godly sorrow for sin, is an essential element in Christian living, rising from a constant awareness of one's inadequate performance of religious duties and the carnal way of handling daily affairs. This sense of sinfulness "will every day of your lives suggest matter for sorrow, for complaint, and for self-accusation before God."[7]

The sinner's happiness, he continued, comes from a knowledge of the nature of God, to be found in Christ. As Mediator, the Saviour gives the only "spiritual view of the character and perfections of the blessed God." This happiness consists in "love to God" and a "friendly intercourse" with him.[8]

Now, my brethren, collect all these things together, God's manifestation of himself, in his greatness and glory, in his dominion and majesty, in his mercy and grace, in his faithfulness and all-sufficiency to our souls; and the reciprocal operations of our own hearts toward him, in prostrating our very souls at his feet, as base, depraved, and damnable creatures; depending on his revealed mercy, in the Lord Jesus Christ, as all-sufficient to save the vilest of men; exercising love to them, as thus displayed; casting ourselves

---

5   Booth, *Works*, 3:249.
6   Booth, *Works*, 3:253–304.
7   Booth, *Works*, 3:310.
8   Booth, *Works*, 3:316–319.

upon his care and giving up ourselves to his disposal;—when God thus manifests himself to our souls, and when our souls are thus exercised toward God, this is what the Bible calls *communion with God*; and this is an anticipation of celestial felicity.[9]

Finally, Booth ventures, many who call themselves Christians and say that they hope to go to heaven when they die, have no real religion and could not be happy if they got there.[10]

AN ESSAY ON THE KINGDOM OF CHRIST

The rational principles of dissent from the national religious establishment had been very little discussed among the English Nonconformists until Booth published *An Essay on the Kingdom of Christ* in 1788.[11] Bishop Hoadley had, in 1717, preached a sermon before King George I, using as his text Christ's words to Pilate, "My kingdom is not of this world" (John 18:36). In the sermon, the Bishop undertook to show that the Kingdom of Christ is a spiritual kingdom, and that the church neither did nor could possess the slightest degree of authority under any commission from the King of England. It was a challenge of the divine right of the Episcopacy, and the committee which the Convocation set up to examine the sermon censured it severely. The controversy which it set off ran for years and served to dispel much of the obscurity in the mind of the public relative to the subject and to divest church authority of its domineering form.[12]

Booth's essay is a treatment of the same subject and based upon the same text:

"My kingdom is not of this world." A concise, but comprehensive declaration, and worthy of him that made it!—This captial saying may be considered as the grand maxim on which he formed his conduct when among men; and it is pregnant with needful instruction to all his disciples, respecting the New Economy and the Christian Church.[13]

---

9 Booth, *Works*, 3:319–320.
10 Booth, *Works*, 3:321.
11 "Memoir of the Author" (*Works*, 1:xlvii).
12 "Memoir of the Author" (*Works*, 1:xlviii).
13 Abraham Booth, *An Essay on the Kingdom of Christ* (London, 1788), 9–10.

Pointing out that the gospel church is the kingdom of Christ, Booth contended that its origin, subjects, laws, and external appearances were not of this world.[14] Christ is a spiritual Sovereign, reigning in the minds, consciences, hearts, and behaviour of his subjects, requiring of them spiritual dispositions and spiritual obedience. Only those who are born from above are subjects of Jesus Christ, "for if the heart be not under his dominion, he reigns not at all as a spiritual monarch."[15]

Following a discussion of the kingdom of David and the Jewish theocracy, Booth summarized:

> For Christ has not made an external covenant with any people. He is not the king of any particular nation. He dwells not in a palace made with hands. His throne is in the heavenly sanctuary; nor does he afford his visible Presence in any place upon earth. The partition wall between Jews and Gentiles has long been demolished: and, consequently, our divine Sovereign does not stand related to any people, or to any person, so as to confer a relative sanctuary, or to produce an external holiness.[16]

From this Old Testament background, Booth turned to consider the congregational church of the New Testament, consisting of those who make a credible profession of repentance and faith, and who constitute "the visible kingdom of Christ." Pointing out that the Scripture shows the first churches to be congregational, with no national church for 300 years, it is evident that these state churches, founded on human laws and acknowledging a visible head, either civil or religious, are "secular kingdoms, and unworthy the name of Christian churches."[17]

"The great design of our Lord in founding a Spiritual empire was, to display the perfections of God in the holiness and happiness of his chosen people," Booth explains. This empire is not of secular power and external pomp; but of truth, righteousness, love, and peace. It was erected on the labours of plain, unlettered men, and its military service is of a purely spiritual nature.[18]

Booth attacked vehemently the preachers who, by their pulpit behaviour, seem to forget they are officers in a kingdom not of this world:

---

14 Booth, *Kingdom of Christ*, 11, 13, 58, 64.
15 Booth, *Kingdom of Christ*, 15, 17.
16 Booth, *Kingdom of Christ*, 29.
17 Booth, *Kingdom of Christ*, 36, 37.
18 Booth, *Kingdom of Christ*, 44–46.

Is there any reason to be surprised that men of sense, who are prejudiced against the genuine gospel, should have their disaffection to evangelical truths increased, when they find those truths avowed, and their importance loudly urged, by merryandrews? ...Is there any reason to wonder, that Infidels should thence take occasion to ridicule the Scripture, as calculated to serve the meanest purposes; or that they should contemptuously call preaching, *priestcraft*? If those who profess to love revealed truths dress them up in a fool's coat, for the entertainment of their hearers, will Deists forbear to laugh?[19]

Other evidences of the carnal nature of the national church, Booth stated, were its claims to power to decree rites or ceremonies, as though Christ was not the lawmaker for his own kingdom.[20] He attacked the Establishment on the subjects of its sanctuaries, dress, and ceremonies:

It must therefore be very absurd to think of doing honour to Christianity, by erecting *pompous places* of worship, by *consecrating* those places, and by adorning ministers with *showy vestments*, in the performance of public worship ...Were any man to lacker gold, and paint the diamond, to increase their luster, he would certainly be considered as insane. Yet the conduct of those persons is more absurd, who borrow the trappings of secular kingdoms, to adorn the spiritual kingdom of Jesus Christ.

As to *places of worship*, conveniency is all that is wanted, and all that becomes the simplicity of Christianity. To lay the first stone of such an edifice with solemn formalities, is Jewish: to dedicate it, when completed, to any particular saint, is manifestly superstitious: to consecrate it by any solemn form, looks as if it succeeded to the honours of Solomon's temple; as if the Deity were expected to reside in it, rather than grant his presence to the congregation worshipping there; and as if it were to possess a relative holiness, like that of the ancient sanctuary. I may venture to add, that any religious parade at the first opening of such a place, is apparently inconsistent with the idea of all distinction of places in regard to worship, being abolished, and too much resembles a Jewish, or a Popish consecration.[21]

The author further disparaged the clerical dress, pomposity in the pulpit, and ecclesiastical ritual which were to be found in the national church:

19   Booth, *Kingdom of Christ*, 56–57.
20   Booth, *Kingdom of Christ*, 63.
21   Booth, *Kingdom of Christ*, 65–66.

That God be adored in Spirit and in truth, according to his own rule, is all it requires of one congregation or another ...Though far from supposing rusticity, illiteracy and meanness, to be characteristics of a Gospel church; yet I may venture to assert, that an assembly of princes in a splendid cathedral, with an archprelate appearing in canonical pomp, may insult the Divine Majesty, and be utterly unworthy the name of a church; while a congregation of day-labourers, with an illiterate minister in the meanest habit, convened in a barn, may be a spiritual temple, enjoy the Divine Presence, and perform the Christian worship in all its glory.[22]

John Carter of Mattishall published in 1806, *An Enquiry into the Origin, Nature, and Administration of Messiah's Kingdom*, in which he questioned the opinions of Booth, along with other writers. This was the nearest thing to a reply to Booth's essay which appeared. Carter criticized Booth for his understanding of the nature of the covenant at Sinai and classed him with Erskine, J. Edwards, and Warburton as a seeming Socinian in this connection.[23]

COMMERCE IN THE HUMAN SPECIES

Reference was made in Chapter 4 to Booth's protest against slavery, *Commerce in the Human Species, and the Enslaving of Innocent Persons, Inimical to the Laws of Moses and the Gospel of Christ*, and the influence this sermon enjoyed in Britain and America. Based on the text, "He that stealeth a man and selleth him, or if he be found in his hand, he shall surely be put to death" (Exodus 21:16), the sermon is a comparison of slavery as practiced by the ancient Hebrews and that of the eighteenth-century British.

The justifications for enslaving an Israelite, Booth pointed out, were theft and insolvency.[24] In respect to the enslavement of neighbouring peoples, permitted by Jehovah, the author stated, as Creator of all things, Jehovah could make them examples of his justice, that his chosen people and others, in distant countries, "might learn to revere his righteous government, and stand in awe of his terrible judgments." Booth inquired as to "what nation in Europe has the least pretence to

---

22 Booth, *Kingdom of Christ*, 71.

23 John Carter, *An Enquiry into the Origin, Nature, and Administration of Messiah's Kingdom, &c.* (Norwich: Stevenson and Matchett, 1806).

24 Booth, *Works*, 3:191.

a divine grant of any particular district on the African continent?"[25] A further distinction was in the handling of Caananitish bond-servants who were protected from cruelty by divine law. English Colonial law, however, afforded the Negro no such protection.[26]

The only authorities for European man-stealing that Booth could find were those of power, policy, or inclination. "It would, consequently, be quite as equitable, benevolent, and humane, for the Africans, laden with produce of their own country, annually to visit our English ports, as we do theirs, and for similar purposes."[27]

The author declared flatly that slavery was utterly opposed to the principles and doctrine of Christ, as witnessed in his commands to "Love your enemies," "Do good to them that hate you," "All things whatsoever ye would that men should do to you, do ye even so to them." Thus, the perpetrators of the system stand condemned, whether involved in the stealing, buying, or enslaving an innocent man.[28]

Booth urged that "zeal for the honour of Christ, and love to our fellow-creatures, ought therefore to inspire us with ardent prayer, that the horrid impediment may be removed, and that Christ may be glorified among them." He further urged that prayer be augmented by "prudent, peaceable, and steady efforts" to abolish the slave traffic entirely, as Christ enjoined, "Thou shalt love thy neighbour as thyself."[29]

THE AMEN TO SOCIAL PRAYER

The Baptist Monthly Meeting took as a series of sermons the Lord's Prayer (Matthew 6:9–13). It fell to Abraham Booth to conclude the "exercise" with a discussion of the final word, "Amen," after his colleagues had considered the prayer itself in detail. He used the opportunity to build upon this one word text a thorough treatise on prayer.

> ...our Amen, whether in public or in private, is a mere formality, if we do not pay a solemn regard to the Amen of God himself; so it manifestly teaches the necessity of praying according to the divine revealed will. For why do we pray, if not that God may regard, approve, and accept our

---

25 Booth, *Works*, 3:197, 199.
26 Booth, *Works*, 3:200.
27 Booth, *Works*, 3:203.
28 Booth, *Works*, 3:206, 207, 213.
29 Booth, *Works*, 3:214, 215.

adorations, confessions, petitions, and thanksgivings, that are addressed to him? which there is no reason to expect, except in proportion as our prayers are conformable to his own directions.[30]

Booth admonished his hearers to use the means God appointed for their spiritual improvement, and to put their prayers into practice, if they expected God to say "Amen" to their petitions. "It is a good saying of an eminent author," Booth quoted, "He who prays as he ought, will endeavour to live as he prays."[31]

This "Amen" suggested to Booth necessary cautions and reproofs to the one who leads the worship, those who join in silently and those who habitually take the lead.[32] He condemned:

The use of such words and modes of speech as his fellow-worshippers do not understand... Never is a desire of appearing learned, or of having the command of elegant language, so misapplied, so contemptible, and so abominable in the sight of God, as when addressing him in public prayer.[33]

There is no place for controversy in social prayer, Booth reasoned, if all are to be able to unite in the "Amen." Such a requirement absolutely excludes "every appearance of angry, envious, and malevolent passions."[34] Prayer, on the other hand, is adapted:

...To maintain on the mind a devout sense of our entire dependence on God; of his dominion over us; and of our accountableness to him, as the Moral Governor of the world—To excite reverence of his majesty, his justice, and his purity—To promote the exercise of self-abasement, of contrition, or of godly sorrow for sin, before him—To endear the atonement and intercession of Jesus; being conscious that we are sinners, and knowing that he, to whom we pray, *is a consuming fire*—To increase our desire of sanctifying influence, and of conformity to the Redeemer's image—To prepare our hearts for a thankful reception of the blessings that are necessary for us.—To promote, by interceding for others, the exercise of brotherly love, to real Christians; and of the social, benevolent affections, toward all mankind—To habituate and familiarize ourselves in filial communion with God—To be a means of enjoying those heavenly

---

30 Booth, *Works*, 3:104.
31 Booth, *Works*, 3:113.
32 Booth, *Works*, 3:114, 120, 128.
33 Booth, *Works*, 3:115.
34 Booth, *Works*, 3:117, 118.

foretastes, those refined pleasures, which nothing but fellowship with the Father and the Son can possibly afford—To prepare us, as well for arduous duties, as for painful conflicts, here; and to mature us for a joyful departure hence into the state of celestial blessedness.[35]

Evidence of Abraham Booth's peculiar fitness to speak on prayer lies in the report of an American physician, visiting in London, who attended Booth's worship services and commented:

> I have heard your famous Mr. Booth today; I assure you I was highly gratified—not peculiarly with his sermon, though I was pleased with that; but I was charmed with his prayer. I have frequently thought that our ministers sometimes pray with wisdom without warmth, and some of them with warmth without wisdom; but I do not recollect to have been struck, at any time, with such a union of both, as I observed in him today. When I return, it will be a pleasure to me to assure our president and the students, that in England I have heard several ministers preach, but that I have heard one minister pray.[36]

PASTORAL CAUTIONS

In 1785, Booth delivered his *Pastoral Cautions* at the ordination of Thomas Hopkins. In 1805, after fifty years in the ministry, he was eminently qualified to publish this practical work on ministerial character and work. It is not an address on homiletics, but of sound instructions on the behaviour of ministers, drawn from the text, "Take heed to thyself" (1 Timothy 4:16).

The elderly pastor cautioned his young colleague to take heed:

> ...with regard to the reality of true godliness, and the state of religion in your own soul; ...lest you mistake an increase of gifts for a growth in grace; ...that your pastoral office prove not a snare to your soul, by lifting you up with pride and self-importance; ...respecting your temper and conduct in general; ...beware of covetousness...to your second-self, in the person of your wife...with regard to the diligent improvement of your talents and opportunities, in the whole course of your ministry; ...respecting

---

35 Booth, *Works*, 3:134.
36 Quoted Ernest F. Kevan, *London's Oldest Baptist Church (Wapping 1633–Walthamstow 1933)* (London: Kingsgate Press, 1933), 129, from Little Prescott Street Church Minutes.

the motives by which you are influenced in all your endeavours to obtain useful knowledge.[37]

Reminding the young man that his work is ministerial, not legislative, Booth said:

…you are not a lord in the church, but a servant…the New Testament attaches no honour to the character of a pastor, except in connection with his humility and benevolence, his diligence and zeal, in promoting the cause of the Great Shepherd—and, that there is no character upon earth which so ill accords with a proud, imperious, haughty spirit, as that of a Christian pastor.[38]

Booth warned against taking offence in the face of criticisms of any kind, explaining that such irritation, while it may accompany ability or success in the ministry, would "be an evidence of pride, and of your being, as a *Christian*, in a poor, feeble state." In instances of opposition from church members, he advised, "endeavour, as it were, to *levy a tax* upon these trials; that they may, at least, afford private advantage to your own soul—and, then, leaving your cause with God, *be of good courage*."[39]

In the realm of finances, Booth advised the young man to seek to provide the necessities of life, without going into debt, living if possible, sufficiently within his income "to spare something for the poor." A pastor should guard against entering unnecessarily into secular employment or accepting any trust in which he is called upon to manage property. He reminds that Christ's kingdom is not of this world, and thus, "it cannot be either adorned by riches, or disgraced by poverty."[40]

A reviewer in the *Evangelical Magazine* calls *Pastoral Cautions* a "modest title" for such a splendid work which merits "the attention of every young pastor in the kingdom," even though the admonitions had been delivered long before.[41] In a *Baptist Magazine* article entitled, "Mr. Booth's Conversational Advice and Remarks," the writer calls it "a work which every pastor should possess, and which every one who assists at the ordination of young ministers should exhort them to purchase, as

---

37 Kevan, *London's Oldest Baptist Church*, 142, 143, 145, 147, 149, 153, 157, 158.
38 Kevan, *London's Oldest Baptist Church*, 145.
39 Kevan, *London's Oldest Baptist Church*, 146, 175.
40 Kevan, *London's Oldest Baptist Church*, 151, 152, 153.
41 "Pastoral Cautions", *The Evangelical Magazine*, 13 (1805):229.

next in point of excellence to the Epistles of Paul to Timothy and Titus."[42]

Booth's own refreshing humility, the like of which he repeatedly urged in *Pastoral Cautions*, is revealed in his reaction to criticism from one of his members of his preaching. The member indicated that his pastor failed to touch on certain articles of which he happened to be very fond, and that he could not profit by Mr. Booth's ministry as he wished. Booth paused awhile, then meekly said, "Ah, brother! So far am I from being astonished at your not profiting under my ministry, that I often feel amazed at God's making me useful to anybody at all."[43]

POSTHUMOUS ESSAYS

At the time of his death, Booth had three essays ready for publication, after another revision. The one entitled "Evidences of Faith in Jesus Christ both Negatively and Positively Considered" written years before, had been revised and enlarged. In 1813 it was published, along with two other essays—"On the Love of God to His Chosen People" and "On a Conduct and Character Formed Under the Influence of Divine Truth"—as he had prepared them, with the exception of a few words changed by W. Button in the unfinished manuscript on faith.[44] In the first essay, "On the Love of God to His Chosen People," Booth distinguished divine love in the following:

> Mercy, grace, and love, when ascribed by inspired writers to the Most High, are to be considered as different modifications of divine goodness; and they may be thus distinguished. Mercy is goodness to the miserable; grace is goodness to the *unworthy*; and love is goodness *delighting in the happiness of its objects*.[45]

This love, he described further, as free, wise, fervent, holy in design and means, steadfast, and "most certain of obtaining its end."[46]

The author agrees with the Scriptural representation of God's gift of his only begotten Son, as "the strongest expression, and the brightest

---

42 *The Baptist Magazine*, 2 (1810):18.

43 Kevan, *London's Oldest Baptist Church*, 128–129.

44 Abraham Booth, *Posthumous Essays, with Confession of Faith* (London: W. Button, 1808), 111.

45 Booth, *Works*, 3:328.

46 Booth, *Works*, 3:330 ff.

evidence of God's love to mankind, that ever blessed and astonished the world."[47]

The second essay, "On a Conduct and Character Formed Under the Influence of Evangelical Truth," asserts "A sincere affection to God will manifest itself, by keeping his commands; to Christ, by imitating his examples; to saints, by treating them as his members; and to our neighbours in common, by a readiness to do them good."[48] There is no scriptural evidence that unregenerate man would ever have loved God or desired to show him honour, if the Father had not revealed his pardoning mercy.[49] Only those who are disposed to pity and relieve their fellow-creatures qualify as real saints, and the Christian needs a lowliness of mind to recognize "there is not a duty of spiritual love that unbecomes them." In this connection, Booth maintained, "The New Testament knows nothing of real Christians that are habitually of a selfish, envious and contentious temper." Divine grace, however, is as fully adapted to subdue such tempers as it is to deliver them from sensual sin.[50] "Ye must be born again," Booth concludes and declares, "Our treasure must be in heaven, and our affections on things above, if we mean either to live comfortably here, or to be happy hereafter."[51]

In his third essay, Booth explored "Evidences of Faith in Jesus Christ, Both Negatively and Positively Considered." He called attention to the fact that a mere desire of grace is not to be considered grace, or that wishing to believe is believing. One's emotional rapture or lack of it is not a sure sign of belief or unbelief.[52] In proof, he gave his personal testimony:

In regard to the general course of my own experience, I must confess, that my peace and comfort, respecting an interest in Christ, have not arisen so much from any *particular* promise; as from a *more general view* of the covenant of grace—of the gospel of peace—of the design of our Lord's mediation—of his all-sufficiency, suitableness, and freeness—of the assurances he gives that those who trust in him shall not be disappointed— of the consciousness I have that I do trust in him—and from some other

---

47 Booth, *Works*, 3:336.
48 Booth, *Works*, 3:350.
49 Booth, *Works*, 3:351.
50 Booth, *Works*, 3:362 ff.
51 Booth, *Works*, 3:371.
52 Booth, *Works*, 3:377–379.

considerations which are more immediately adapted to prove that my faith is genuine. This, I presume, is the case with multitudes of real Christians.[53]

After enumerating those things which are *not* criteria for real belief, such as terror, followed by peace of conscience, extensive knowledge of spiritual gifts, or usefulness in ministerial employ, he explained that the reverse—lack of terror, doctrinal ignorance, some wrong views, inability to pray in public, etc., are not necessarily evidence of a lost condition.[54]

Booth concludes by stating, as the genuine evidence of faith:

> He who really believes in Jesus Christ, *cordially and habitually depends upon him, for pardon and peace, for righteousness and strength*...He who truly believes on the Son of God, *habitually and cordially approves* the way of salvation by Jesus Christ, as being not only *safe*, with regard to the sinner, but *worthy* of God, as becoming his character.[55]

---

53 Booth, *Works*, 3:383.
54 Booth, *Works*, 3:385–386.
55 Booth, *Works*, 3:387.

THE COMPLETE WORKS OF ABRAHAM BOOTH

An Address Delivered to Joshua Marshman, William Ward, D. Brunsdon, and W. Grant, on Their Departure to India. (n.p.): McIntyre 1799.

The Amen to Social Prayer. A Sermon; London, 1801.

  Another edition; London: W. Button, 1813.

An Apology for the Baptists. London: E. & C. Dilly, 1778.

  Another edition; With *An Apology for the Bible to Thomas Paine.*
    Boston: Manning and Loring, 1796.
  Another edition; Philadelphia: Thomas Dobson, 1788.
  Another edition; London, 1812.
  Another edition; Boston: Manning and Loring, 1808.

A Charge and Sermon, Confession of Faith. London: G. Keith, 1769.

  Another edition; *Posthumous Essays, to Which is Annexed Booth's
    Confession of Faith, Delivered at his Ordination in Goodman's*

Fields, February 16, 1769. London: W. Button, 1808

A Charge to Francis Smith and Thomas Perkins at Melbourne. (Perhaps not published).

The Christian Triumph. An address at the interment of Miss Ann Williams; London: E. & C. Dilly, 1772.

> Another edition; London: E. & C. Dilly, 1773.
> Another edition; London: W. Button; T. Knott, 1796.
> Another edition; Abridged; Haddington, 1806.
> Another edition; Bound with *The Death of Legal Hope.* Translated into Dutch from English by Marinus van Werkhoven. Second edition; Rotterdam, 1776.

Commerce in the Human Species, and the Enslaving of Innocent Persons Inimical to the Laws of Moses and the Gospel of Christ. A Sermon. London: C. Dilly/T. Knott, 1792.

> Another edition; Translated into Dutch from English by Marinus van Werkhoven, Amsterdam, 1790.
> Another edition, third; London, 1792.
> Another; Philadelphia: Daniel Lawrence, 1792.

The Death of Legal Hope, The Life of Evangelical Obedience. An Essay on Galatians 2:19. London: E. & C. Dilly, 1770.

> Another edition; With *The Christian Triumph.* Translated into Dutch from English by Marinus van Werkhoven; Second edition; Rotterdam, 1776.
> Another edition; London: J. Johnson, 1778.
> Another edition; London: W. Button, 1794.
> Another edition; With *Glad Tidings.* Carlisle, Pennsylvania: A. Loudon, 1805.

Another edition; Boston: Manning and Loring, 1806.
Another edition; London: Button, 1811.
Another edition; (n.p.): 1823.
Another edition; With *Reign of Grace* and *Glad Tidings*. In *Select Works*; London: 1839.
Another edition; In Vol. III of *The Baptist Library: A Republication of Standard Baptist Works*, eds. Charles G. Sommers, William R. Williams, and Levi L. Hill (New York: Lewis Colby & Co., 1846)

A Defence of Paedobaptism Examined; or Animadversions on Dr. Edward Williams's AntiPaedobaptism Examined. London, 1792.

The Deity of Jesus Christ Essential to the Christian Religion: A Treatise on the Divinity of Our Lord Jesus Christ, by James Abbadie. A new edition of the English translation, revised, corrected, and in a few places abridged by Abraham Booth. (n.p.): J. Harris, 1777.

Another edition; In *The Doctrinal Puritans and Divines of the 17th Century*. Vol. XIII; 18 vols.; London: The Religious Tract Society (Instituted 1799), (n.d.).
Another edition; Charlestown: A. Brown, 1817.
Another edition; (n.p.): 1838.

Divine Justice Essential to the Divine Character: A Sermon, &c. London, 1804.
Another edition; (n.p.): 1803.

Encouragements and Cautions for the Household of Faith. London, 1897.

An Essay on the Kingdom of Christ. London, 1788.

Another edition; New York: W. Durrell, 1791.
Another edition; With *The Doctrine of the Covenants*, by Samuel Jones. Norwich, 1801.

Another edition; Edited by John Sterry, Norwhich "True
   Republican," with notes containing his strictures on the
   Connecticut and English Established Church. New London,
   Connecticut, 1801.
Another edition; New Haven, 1802.
Another edition, third; London: W. Button, 1808.
Another edition; Translated into Welsh by David Sanders;
   Aberysthwyth, 1810.
Another edition, from second London edition; Boston: Manning
   and Loring, 1811.
Another edition; (n.p.): 1806.
Another edition, fourth; London, 1813.
Another edition; Bridgeport: Rufus Langdon, 1825.
Another edition; With *Pastoral Cautions*; London: Houlston and
   Stoneman, 1846.
Another edition, sixth; New York: S. Cameron, 1874.
Another edition; London: Houlston and Stoneman, 1846.
Another edition; Translated into Welsh by David Sanders;
   Methyr: (n.d.).

The Faithful Rewarded: An Address at the Interment of Rev. B. Wallin.
London, 1782.

Glad Tidings to Perishing Sinners. London, 1796.

Another edition; Philadelphia, 1797.
Another edition, second; London: W. Button, T. Knott, 1800.
Another edition; Carlisle, Pennsylvania: A. Loudon, 1805.
Another edition; With *The Death of Legal Hope*; Carlisle,
   Pennsylvania: A. Loudon, 1805.
Another edition; (n.p.): 1813.
Another edition, fifth; London: William Jones, 1825.
Another edition; Philadelphia: S. Taylor, 1833.
Another edition; With *Reign of Grace* in condensed form;
   Washington, Ohio, 1831.
Another edition; With *Reign of Grace* and *Death of Legal Hope*, in

Select Works; London, 1839.
Another edition; Aberdeen, 1844.
Another edition; Philadelphia: T. Ustick, (n.d.).

The Love of the Brethren Proceeding from a Perception of the Love of God: Address at the Interment of Rev. Samuel Stennett, 1795. London, 1795.

Notes of Sermons preached at Nottingham, Friar-lane; apparently the raw material for *The Reign of Grace*. George Street Church, 1764.

On Absolute Predestination; a Poem mentioned in *A History of the English Baptist*s, by Joseph Ivimey. Vol. IV; (Rivington) 1760.

Paedobaptism Examined, on the Principles, Concessions, and Reasonings of the Most Learned Paedobaptists. London, 1784.

Another edition, second; 2 vols.; London, 1787.
Another edition; London: Dobson (?), 1788.
Another edition; Abridged and published by Peter Bryant; Newark: 1805.
Another edition, third; 3 vols.; London: Ebenezer Palmer, 1829.
Another edition; In Vol. I of *The Baptist Library: A Republication of Standard Baptist Works*, eds. Charles G. Sommers, William R. Williams, and Levi L. Hill (New York: Lewis Colby & Co., 1846)

Pastoral Cautions: An Address to the Late Mr. Thomas Hopkins, When Ordained Pastor of the Church in Eagle Street, Red Lion Square... 1785. London, 1785.

Another edition; London, 1805.
Another edition, third; With *An Essay on the Kingdom of Christ*. London, 1808.
Another edition; London: W. Button and Son, 1813.
Another edition; (n.p.): 1832.

Another edition; (n.p.): 1836
Another edition; With *An Essay on the Kingdom of Christ.*
London: Houlston and Stoneman, 1846.

Posthumous Essays, To Which is Annexed his Confession of Faith,
Delivered at His Ordination in Goodman's Fields, February 16, 1769.
London: W. Button, 1808.

Principles of AntiPaedobaptism, and the Principles of Female
Communion Completely Consistent; in Reply to Mr. Peter Edwards with
Animadversions on his Temper and his Conduct in that Publication.
Written anonymously, with Preface and Notes by Rev. James Dore;
London, 1795.

The Reign of Grace From its Rise to its Consummation. Leeds: Griffith
Wright, 1768.

> Another edition, second; London: E. & C. Dilly, 1771.
> Another edition; Translated into Dutch from the second English
> edition; Utrecht, 1774.
> Another edition, fourth; London: L. Wayland, 1790.
> Another edition; First American from fourth London edition;
> New York: 1793.
> Another edition; London: Booksellers, 1795.
> Another edition; Burlington, New Jersey, 1795.
> Another edition; Third American from fourth London edition;
> Philadelphia, 1798.
> Another edition; Philadelphia: T. Ustick, (about 1802).
> Another edition, seventh; London: W. Baynes, 1803.
> Another edition, eighth; London: W. Baynes, 1807.
> Another edition; Carlisle, Pennsylvania: A. Loudon, 1807.
> Another edition; With essay on his life and writings by William
> Jones; Liverpool: William Jones, 1808.
> Another edition, second American; New York: John
> Tiebout, 1809.

Another edition; London: J. Bailey, 1810.
Another edition, third American; Hartford: James Hadlock, 1814.
Another edition; London, 1822.
Another edition; Boston: Lincoln and Edmands, 1824.
Another edition; With introductory essay by Thomas Chalmers; Number 39 of *Select Christian Authors*; Glasgow: William Collins, 1828.
Another edition; Washington, Ohio: H. Robb, 1831.
Another edition; With *Glad Tidings*; Washington, Ohio: H. Robb, 1831.
Another edition; London: Book Society for Promoting Religious Knowledge, 1832.
Another edition; Philadelphia: Joseph Whetham, 1838.
Another edition; With a Memoir of his life and writings; Philadelphia: Baptist tract Depository, 1839.
Another edition; With *Glad Tidings* and *Death of Legal Hope*, in *Select Works*; London, 1839.
Another edition; New York: Robert Carter and Brothers, 1856.
Another edition; New York: Robert Carter and Brothers, 1859.
Another edition; New York, 1861.
Another edition; London: F. Kirby, 1887.
Another edition; With memoir and picture; American Baptist Publication Society and Sunday School Society, 1841 (?).
Another edition; With introductory essay by Thomas Chalmers; New York: Robert Carter and Brothers, 1861.
Another edition; Edinburgh: Thomas Nelson, 1844.
Another edition; American Baptist Publication Society, (1908).
Another edition; Phoenix; Philadelphia: American Baptist Publication Society, 1910.
Another edition, third; *The Glorious Triumphs of Grace*, by W. S. Craig; Being mainly an abridgment of *Reign of Grace*; Kearney, Nebraska, 1924.
Another edition; Grand Rapids, Michigan: Eerdmans Publishing Company, 1949.
Another edition; With introductory essay by Thomas Chalmers, first appearance in an American edition; Philadelphia: American Baptist Publication Society, (n.d.).
Another edition; Philadelphia: American Baptist Publication

Society, (n.d.).
Another edition; Corrected by the 16th London edition;
 Philadelphia: American Baptist Publication Society, (n.d.).
Another edition; Philadelphia: American Baptist Publication
 Society, (n.d.).
Another edition; With an introductory essay by Thomas Chalmers,
 from the 16th London edition; Philadelphia; American Baptist
 Publication Society, (n.d.).

The Remembrance of Our Creator: An Address at the Interment of Mr. T.
Wilton, 1776. London, 1776.

A Scripture Manual, or, A Plain Representation of the Ordinance
of Baptism, by Samuel Wilson; Revised by Abraham Booth;
London, 1797.

Another edition; (n.p.), 1824.
Another edition; (n.p.), 1834.

Selections from the Writings of Rev. Abraham Booth, E. Steene, editor; *The*
Bunyan Library; Vol. XVI; London, 1865.

The Sorrowful Separation of the Faithful Pastor from his Affectionate
Flock: Address at the Interment of Mr. J. Swain. 1796.

Vindication of the Baptists from the Charge of Bigotry in Refusing
Communion at the Lord's Table to Paedobaptists. Abridged from Booth's
Works; Philadelphia: American Baptist Publication Society, 1778.

Another edition; In *The Baptist Library;* Vol. I; Prattsville, New
 York: Robert H. Hill, 1843.
Another edition; Philadelphia: American Baptist Publication
 Society, (n.d.).

Another edition; In *The Baptist Manual*; Philadelphia: American
Baptist Publication Society, (n.d.).

*The Works of Abraham Booth, With Some Account of His Life and
Writings.* 3 vols. London: J. Haddon, 1813.

WORKS BY ABRAHAM BOOTH

An Address Delivered to Joshua Marshman, William Ward, D. Brunsdon, and W. Grant on their Departure to India. (n.p.): McIntyre, 1799.

The Amen to Social Prayer. London, 1801 (2 editions).

An Apology for the Baptists. London: E. & C. Dilly, 1778 (6 editions).

A Charge and Sermon, Confession of Faith. London: G. Keith, 1769 (2 editions).

The Christian Triumph. London: E. & C. Dilly, 1772 (5 editions).

Commerce in the Human Species, and the Enslaving of Innocent Persons Inimical to the Laws of Moses and the Gospel of Christ. London: C. Dilly; T. Knott, 1792 (4 editions).

The Death of Legal Hope, The Life of Evangelical Obedience. London: E. & C. Dilly, 1770 (10 editions).

A Defense of Paedobaptism Examined; or Animadversions on Dr. Edward Williams's AntiPaedobaptism Examined. London, 1792.

The Deity of Jesus Christ Essential to the Christian Religion, &c., by James Abbadie. A new edition of the English translation, revised by Abraham Booth. London: J. Harris, 1777 (4 editions).

Divine Justice Essential to the Divine Character: A Sermon, &c. London, 1804 (2 editions).

Encouragements and Cautions for the Household of Faith. London, 1897.

An Essay of the Kingdom of Christ. London, 1788 (15 editions).

The Faithful Rewarded. London, 1782.

Glad Tidings to Perishing Sinners. London, 1796 (12 editions).

The Love of the Brethren Proceeding from a Perception of the Love of God. London, 1795.

Paedobaptism Examined, on the Principles, Concessions, and Reasonings of the Most Learned Paedobaptists. London, 1784 (6 editions).

Pastoral Cautions: An Address to the late Mr. Thomas Hopkins, When Ordained Pastor of the Church in Eagle Street, Red Lion Square... 1785. London, 1805 (7 editions).

Posthumous Essays, with Confession of Faith. London: W. Button, 1808.

Principles of AntiPaedobaptism, and the Principles of Female Communion Completely Consistent. London: W. Button, 1795.

The Reign of Grace, From its Rise to its Consummation. Leeds: Griffith Wright, 1768. (42 editions).

The Remembrance of our Creator. London, 1776.

A Scripture Manual, by Samuel Wilson; Revised by Abraham Booth; London, 1797 (4 editions).

Vindication of the Baptists from the Charge of Bigotry in Refusing Communion at the Lord's Table to Paedobaptists. Abridged; Philadelphia: American Baptist Publication Society, 1778 (4 editions).

GENERAL WORKS

Abbadie, James, *The Deity of Jesus Christ Essential to the Christian Religion.* Translated by Abraham Booth; Burlington, N. J.: Thomas Ustick, 1802.

Abbey, Charles J., *The English Church and Its Bishops, 1700–1800.* 2 vols.; London: Longman's, Green, and Company, 1887.

_____, and John H. Overton, *The English Church in the Eighteenth Century.* London: Longman's, Green, and Company, 1887 and 1902.

Alliborne, S. Austin, *A Critical Dictionary of English Literature and English and American Authors.* Philadelphia: J.B. Lippincott Company, 1902.

Aulen, Gustaf, *Christus Victor.* Translated by A.G. Herbert; New York: The Macmillan Company, 1945.

Baldwin, Thomas, *The Baptism of Believers Only and the Particular Communion of the Baptist Churches.* Second edition; Boston: Manning and Loring, 1806.

Barth, Karl, *The Teaching of the Church Regarding Baptism.* Translated by E.A. Payne, London: S.C.M. Press, 1948.

Bogue, David, and James Bennett, *History of Dissenters from the Revolution in 1688, to the Year 1808.* 4 vols.; London, 1808.

Brown, J. Newton, editor, *History of the American Baptist Publication Society, from its Origin in 1824 to its Thirty-second Anniversary in 1856.* Philadelphia: American Baptist Publication Society, 1856.

Brunner, Emil, *The Christian Doctrine of God. Dogmatics.* Vol. I; translated by Olive Wyon; London: Lutterworth Press, 1949.

_____, *The Divine-Human Encounter.* Translated by Amandus W. Loos; London: S.C.M. Press, 1944.

_____, *The Mediator.* Translated by Olive Wyon; Philadelphia: The Westminster Press, 1947.

Bryan, F.C. and R.L. Child, *Concerning Believer's Baptism.* London: The Kingsgate Press, 1943.

Calvin, John, *Institutes of the Christian Religion.* Sixth American edition; Philadelphia: Presbyterian Board of Publication, (n.d.).

Carey, S. Pearce, *William Carey.* Eighth edition; London: The Carey Press, 1934.

Carlile, J.C., *The Story of the English Baptists.* London: James Clarke and Company, 1905.

Carson, Alexander, *Baptism in Its mode and Subjects.* Fifth American edition; (n.p.): American Baptist Publication Society, 1850.

Carter, John, *An Enquiry into the Origin, Nature, and Administration of Messiah's Kingdom, &c.* Norwich: Stevenson and Matchett, (Preface date, 1806).

Cathcart, William, *The Baptist Encyclopaedia.* Philadelphia: Louis H. Everts, 1881.

Christian, John T., *Baptist History Vindicated.* Louisville, Kentucky: Baptist Book Concern, 1899.

_____, *A History of the Baptists.* Nashville, Tennessee: Sunday School Board of the Southern Baptist Convention, 1922.

_____, *A History of the Baptists of the United States from the First Settlement of the Country to the Year 1845.* Nashville, Tennessee: Sunday School Board of the Southern Baptist Convention, 1926.

Clifford, John, editor, *The English Baptists, Who They Are, and What They Have Done.* London: E. Marlborough & Co., 1881.

Coles, Thomas, *Advice to Students and Ministers*. Oxford: Bristol Education Society, &c., 1813.

Conant, H.C., *The Earnest Man: A Memoir of Adoniram Judson, D.D.* Vol. III, *The Bunyan Library*; London: J. Heaton and Son, 1861.

Cook, Richard B., *The Story of the Baptists in All Ages and Countries*. (n.p.): R.H. Woodward and Company, 1889.

Coomer, Duncan, *English Dissent Under the Early Hanoverians*, London: The Epworth Press, 1946.

Craig, W.S., *The Glorious Triumphs of Grace*. Third edition; Kearney, Nebraska:, 1924.

Cullmann, Oscar, *Baptism in the New Testament*. Translated by J.K.S. Reid, London: S.C.M. Press, Ltd., 1950.

Culross, James, *The Three Rylands*. London: Elliot Stock, 1897.

Cyclopaedia of Biblical Theological and Ecclesiastical Literature. Vol. I; New York, 1891.

Dakin, A., *Calvinism*. Philadelphia: The Westminster Press, 1946.

Dale, James W., *Classic Baptism*. Second edition; Philadelphia: William Rutter and Company, 1868.

Dale, R.W. *The Atonement*. London: Congregational Union of England and Wales, 1888.

Denney, James, *The Death of Christ*. New York: A.C. Armstrong and Son, 1902.

Dictionary of National Biography, edited by Stephen and Lee. Vol. II; London: Smith, Elder and Company, 1908.

Dodd, C.H., *The Epistle of Paul to the Romans. The Moffett New Testament Commentary*; New York: Harper & Brothers Publishers, (Preface date 1932).

Dore, James, *A Sermon Occasioned by the Death of Abraham Booth.* London: C. Wittingham, 1806.

Dwight, Henry Otis, *The Centennial History of the American Bible Society.* New York: The Macmillan Company, 1916.

Dyer, George, *Memoirs of the Life and Writings of Robert Robinson.* London: G.G. and J. Robinson, 1796.

Edwards, Peter, *Candid Reasons for Renouncing the Principles of Antipaedo-baptism.* Philadelphia: Presbyterian Board of Publication, 1841.

The Eighteenth Century. Vol. VI, *The Cambridge Modern History*; Cambridge: The University Press, 1909.

Elliot, R., *The Consistent Protestant: or The Harmony of Divine Truth Asserted*: &c. London, 1777.

_____, *Dipping not Baptizing or the Author's Opinion of the Subject, Mode and Importance of Water Baptism According to the Scriptures: &c.* London, 1787.

The Encyclopedia Americana. Vol. IV; New York, 1946.

Encyclopaedia Britannica. Vol. III; (n.p.): 1947.

Encyclopedia of Religion and Ethics, Edited by James Hastings; New York: Charles Scribner's Sons, 1926.

The Encyclopaedia of Sunday Schools and Religious Education. (n.p.: n.d.).

The Evangelical Preacher: or a Select Collection of Doctrinal and Practical Sermons, Chiefly by English Divines of the Eighteenth Century. Vol. III; Edinburgh: Ogle and Aiken, 1806.

An Examination of the Rev. Mr. Elliot's Opinion Respecting the Mode of Baptism and the Scriptures on Which it is Founded, &c. London, 1788.

Flemington, W. F., *The New Testament Doctrine of Baptism.* London: S.P.C.K., 1948.

Forsyth, Peter Taylor, *The Work of Christ.* New York: Hodder and Stoughton, 1938.

Fox, William, *Address to the Friends of Evangelical Truth in General, and to the Calvinistic Baptist Churches in Particular.* (n.p.): 1797.

Frey, J. S., *Essays on Christian Baptism.* Fifth edition; New York, 1843.

Fuller, Andrew, *Complete Works.* Edited by Joseph Belcher; 3 vols.; Philadelphia: American Baptist Publication Society, 1845.

_____, *Memoir of Rev. Samuel Pearce, A.M.* New York: American Tract Society; (n.d.).

_____, *Remarks on Manuscript Remarks by Dr. Hopkins on Mr. Booth's Glad Tidings.* (n.p.): 1797.

Fuller, A.G., editor, *The Complete Works of the Rev. Andrew Fuller.* 5 vols.; London: Holdsworth and Ball, 1831.

Fuller, T.E., *A Memoir of the Life and Writings of Andrew Fuller.* London: J. Heaton & Son, 1863.

"General Baptist Assembly," *Annual Proceedings.* 4 vols.; (n.p.): 1771–1868.

Gould, George P., *The Baptist College at Regent's Park.* London: Kingsgate Press, 1910.

Green, J.R., *History of the English People.* 8 vols.; London: Macmillan and Company, 1896.

Gutteridge, Joseph, *Autograph Address, Prepared for the Opening of Stepney College.* (n.p.): 1810.

Hall, Robert (elder), *Help to Zion's Travellers.* Third edition; London: Whittingham and Rowland, 1815.

Hastings, James, *Encyclopaedia of Religion and Ethics.* Vol. II; New York: Charles Scribner's Sons, 1910.

Haynes, D.C., *The Baptist Denomination: its History, Doctrines, and Ordinances.* New York: Sheldon, Blakeman and Company, 1856.

Heppe, Heinrich, *Reformed Dogmatics.* English translation by G.T. Thomson; London: George Allen & Unwin Ltd., 1950.

Higgins, A.J.B., *The Lord's Supper in the New Testament.* London: The S. C.M. Press, 1952.

Hinton, Isaac Taylor, *A History of Baptism.* Revised by John Howard Hinton; London: J. Heaton & Son, 1864.

Howell, Rev. Robert Boyte C., *Terms of Sacramental Communion.* Philadelphia: American Baptist Publication and Sunday School Society, 1841.

Hughes, T.H., *The Atonement.* London: George Allen & Unwin Ltd., 1949.

Ingham, R., *A Handbook on Christian Baptism.* London: Simpkin, Marshall and Company, 1865.

Ivimey, Joseph, *A History of the English Baptists.* 4 vols.; London: Isaac Taylor Hinton, 1830.

_____, *Memoir of William Fox, Esq., Founder of the Sunday School Society: &c.* (n.p.): Wightman, 1831.

Jenkins, Joseph, *A Defence of the Baptists Against the Aspersions and Misrepresentation of Mr. Peter Edwards, &c.* Halifax: Jesse Read and Richard Poindexter, 1805.

Jones, William, Christian Biography: *A Dictionary of the Lives and Writings of the Most Distinguished Christians, &c.* (n.p.): 1829.

_____, *An Essay on the Life and Writings of Abraham Booth.* Liverpool: W. Button, 1808.

Judson, Adoniram, *A Sermon on Christian Baptism.* Fifth American edition, revised and enlarged by author; Boston: Bould, Kendall and Lincoln, 1846.

Julian, John, *A Dictionary of Hymnology.* London: John Murray, 1892.

Kevan, Ernest F., *London's Oldest Baptist Church (Wapping 1633– Walthamstow 1933).* London: Kingsgate Press, 1933.

Kingsbury, T.B., *What is Baptism?* Petersburg, Virginia, 1867.

Lawson, J. Gilchrist, *Did Jesus Command Immersion?* Cincinnati, Ohio: The Standard Publishing Company, 1915.

Lecky, William Edward Hartpole, *A History of England in the Eighteenth Century.* Cabinet edition; 7 vols.; London: Longmans, Green and Company, 1892.

Lloyd, Walter, *Protestant Dissent and English Unitarianism.* London: Philip Green, 1899.

The Lord's Supper, A Baptist Statement. London: The Carey Kingsgate Press, Ltd., 1951.

Luther, Martin, *A Commentary Upon the Epistle of Paul to the Galatians.* [Philadelphia]: Salmon S. Miles, 1837.

Macaulay, Lord, *The History of England from the Accession of James the Second.* 6 vols.; London: Macmillan and Company, Ltd., 1813.

Marcel, P.C., *The Biblical Doctrine of Infant Baptism, Sacrament of the Covenant of Grace.* Translated by Philip Edgcumbe Hughes; London: James Clarke & Co. Ltd., 1953.

Marsh, H.G., *The Origin and Significance of the New Testament Baptism.* Manchester: Manchester University Press, 1941.

Marshman, John Clark, *The Life and Times of Carey, Marshman, and Ward.* Vol. I; London: Longman, Browne, Green, Longmans, and Roberts, 1859.

Mathieson, W.L., *England in Transition, 1789–1832.* London: Longmans, Green and Company, 1920.

McGlothlin, W.J., *Baptist Confessions of Faith.* Philadelphia: American Baptist Publication Society, 1911.

Miller, William, *Catholic Baptism Examined or Thoughts on the Ground and Extent of Baptismal Administration, &c.* High-Wycombe, 1793.

Morris, J.W., *Memoir of the Life and Writings of the Rev. Andrew Fuller.* First American edition from the last London edition; Rufus Babcock, Jun., editor; Boston: Lincoln and Edmands, 1830.

Moss, C.B., *The Christian Faith.* London: Society for Promoting Christian Knowledge, 1943.

Newman, A.H., *A History of the Baptist Churches in the United States.* New York: The Christian Literature Company, 1894.

Newman, William, *Baptism an Indispensable Prerequisite to Communion at the Lord's Table.* (n.p.): 1805.

_____, *The Work and Reward of Faithful Deacons.* London: Button, 1806.

Orchard, G.H., *A History of the Baptists in England.* J.R. Graves, editor; Vol. II; Nashville, Tennessee: Southwestern Publishing House, 1860.

Overton, J.H., *The Church in England.* 2 vols.; London: Gardner, Darton and Company, 1897.

_____, *The English Church in the Nineteenth Century.* London: Longmans and Company, 1894.

_____, *The Evangelical Revival in the Eighteenth Century.* London: Longmans, Green and Company, 1886.

_____, and Frederic Relton, *The English Church from the Accession of George I to the End of the Eighteenth Century (1714–1800).* London: Macmillan and Company, Ltd., 1906.

Owen, John, *Works.* Edited by the Rev. William H. Gould; Vol. V; Philadelphia: Leighton Publication, 1862.

A Paedobaptist, Thoughts on Baptism and Mixed Communion in Three Letters to a Friend in Which Some Animadversions Are Made on the Rev. A. Booth's Apology. Norwich: Stevenson and Matchett, (n.d.).

Payne, E.A., *The Fellowship of Believers, Baptist Thought and Practice Yesterday and Today.* London: Kingsgate Press, 1944.

_____, *The First Generation.* London: Carey Press, 1936 (in Foreword).

_____, *The Free Church Tradition in the Life of England.* Second edition; London: S.C.M. Press, 1944.

Piette, Maximin, *John Wesley in the Evolution of Protestantism.* Translated by the Rev. J.B. Howard; London: Sheed and Ward, 1938.

Price, Seymour J., *A Popular History of the Baptist Building Fund. Centenary Volume, 1824–1924*. London: Kingsgate Press, 1927.

————, *Upton: Story of One Hundred and Fifty Years 1785–1935*. London: The Carey Press, 1935.

Pritchard, George, *Memoir of the Rev. William Newman, D.D.* London: Thomas Ward and Company, 1837.

Rippon, John, *Memorial Sermon for Abraham Booth*. (n.p.): 1806.

Robinson, H. Wheeler, *The Life and Faith of the Baptists*. L. P. Jacks, editor, *The Faiths*; London: Methuen and Company, Ltd., 1927.

Rogers, James E. Thorold, *Six Centuries of Work and Wages: The History of English Labour*. London: Swan Sonnenschein and Company, 1908.

Ryland, John, *The Life and Death of the Rev. Andrew Fuller*. Charlestown: Samuel Etheridge, 1818.

Seymour, Aaron Crossley Hobart, *The Life and Times of Selina Countess of Huntingdon*. Vols. I–II; London: William Edward Painter, 1841–1844.

Shakespeare, J.H., *Baptist and Congregational Pioneers*. London: The Kingsgate Press, 1906.

Sherston, Thomas, *Discourse on the Character of God as Love*. Glasgow, 1805.

————, *Scriptural Subjection to Civil Government: in an Exhortation, &c.* (n.p.): 1794.

Simon, John S., *The Revival of Religion in England in the Eighteenth Century*. 37th Fernley Lecture. London: Charles H. Kelly, (n.d.).

Skeats, H.S., *A History of the Free Churches of England, From 1688–1831.* London: Arthur Miall, 1868.

_____, and C.S. Miall, *History of Free Churches of England, 1688–1891.* London: Alexander and Shepheard, 1891.

Smith, George, *The Life of William Carey, D.D.* London: John Murray, 1855.

Sommers, Williams, and Hill, editors, *The Baptist Library, A Republication of Standard Baptist Works.* Vols. I–III; Prattsville, New York: Robert H. Hill, 1843.

Stennett, Samuel, *Sermon at the Ordination of Abraham Booth, February 16, 1769.* (n.p.:n.d.).

Strong, A.H., *Outlines of Systematic Theology.* Philadelphia: The Griffith & Rowland Press, 1908.

Sydney, W.C., *England and the English in the Eighteenth Century.* 2 vols.; London: Ward and Downey, 1891.

Taylor, Adam, *The History of the English General Baptists.* 2 vols.; London, 1818.

_____, *Memoirs of the Rev. Dan Taylor, &c.* (n.p.): 1820.

Taylor, C., *Apostolic Baptism—Facts and Evidences on the Subjects and Mode of Christian Baptism.* New York: M.W. Dodd, 1850.

Torbet, Robert G., *A History of the Baptists.* Philadelphia: The Judson Press, 1950.

Trevelyan, G. M., *British History in the Nineteenth Century.* London: Longmans, Green and Company, 1922.

Tyerman, Luke, *The Life of the Rev. George Whitefield.* 2 vols.; London: Hodder and Stoughton, 1890.

_____, *The Life and Times of the Rev. John Wesley, M.A. Founder of the Methodists*. 3 vols.; New York: Harper and Brothers, 1872.

Underwood, A.C., *A History of the English Baptists*. London: Kingsgate Press, 1947.

Vedder, Henry C., *The Story of the Churches: The Baptists*. New York: The Baker and Taylor Company, 1903.

Venn, Henry, *The Complete Duty of Man*. New York: American Tract Society, (n.d.).

W.S., *God All in All, Being a Letter to the Baptist Church Meeting at Goodman's Fields, London, &c*. London, 1770.

Walker, Williston, *A History of the Christian Church*. New York: Charles Scribner's Sons, 1919.

Watson, Philip S., *Let God Be God*. Philadelphia: Muhlenberg Press, 1949.

Wearmouth, Robert F., *Methodism and the Common People of the Eighteenth Century*. London: Epworth Press, 1945.

Wesley, Charles, *The Journal of the Rev. Charles Wesley, M.A.* Thomas Jackson, editor; 2 vols.; London: Wesleyan-Methodist Book-Room, 1849.

Wesley, John, *The Journal of John Wesley*. Standard edition; 8 vols.; London: The Epworth Press, 1938.

_____, *The Works of the Rev. John Wesley, A.M., Sometime Fellow of Lincoln College, Oxford*. Third edition; 14 vols.; London: Wesleyan-Methodist Book-Room, 1831.

Wood, J.H., *A Condensed History of the General Baptists of the New Connexion*. London: Simpkin, Marshall and Company, 1847.

Whitley, W.T., *A Baptist Bibliography*. London: Kingsgate Press, 1916.

_____, *Calvinism and Evangelism in England, Especially in Baptist Circles*. London: Kingsgate Press, 1933.

_____, *A History of British Baptists*. London: Kingsgate Press, 1932.

_____, *The Baptists of London 1612–1928*. London: Kingsgate Press, 1928.

Wilkin, M.H., *Joseph Kinghorn of Norwich*. Norwich: Fletcher and Alexander, 1855.

Williams, Edward, *Antipaedobaptism Examined: or, A Strict and Impartial Inquiry into the Nature and Design, Subjects and Mode of Baptism*. Shrewsbury: 1789.

Yuille, George, editor, *History of the Baptists in Scotland from Prereformation Times*. Glasgow: Baptist Union Publications Committee, 1926.

PAMPHLETS AND PERIODICALS

The American Baptist Magazine, and Missionary Intelligencer. New Series; Vol. IV; Boston: James Loring and Lincoln Edmands, 1823.

The Annual Register for the Year 1792. London: Proprietors of Dodsley's Annual Register, 1799.

The Annual Register for 1793. London: Baldwin, Cradock, and Joy, 1821.

Annual Reports of the American Bible Society with an Account of Its Organization. Vol. I; New York: Reprinted for the Society, 1838.

Arminian Magazine. Vols. I–XX; 1778–1797. The name was then changed to: *The Methodist Magazine*. Vols. XXI–XLIV; 1798–1820.

The Baptist Magazine. Vols. I–III, and VI; London, 1809–1814.

The Baptist Memorial and Monthly Record. Vol. V; New York: J.R. Bigelow, 1846.

"Baptist Missionary Society," *Periodical Accounts No. 1*. 33 numbers; 1794.

The Baptist Quarterly Incorporating the *Transactions of the Baptist Historical Society*. New Series; Vols. I–XII; London: Baptist Union Publication Department, 1922–1947.

Bristol Baptist College, 250 Years—1679–1929. Bristol: Rankin Brothers, Ltd., 1929.

Coles, Thomas, "Election," *Circular of the Oxon at Bourton*, 1833.

_____, "Hindrances to Secret Devotions with the Means of Their Removal", *Circular of the Oxon at Witney*. 1809.

_____, "The Indulgence of Vain Curiosity," *Circular of the Oxon at Astwood*. Chipping Norton, 1816.

The Edinburgh Review for April 1806 to July 1806. Vol. III; Edinburgh: Archibald Constable and Company, 1806.

Elliot, W., "Christian Zeal," *Circular of the Oxon at Fairford*. 1836.

The Evangelical Magazine. Vols. IX–XXI; London, 1801–1813.

The General Baptist Magazine. Four series; London, 1822–1891.

The General Baptist Repository. Adam Taylor, editor; 1802.

Historical Catalogue of Brown University, Providence, R. I., 1764–1894. Providence, R. I.: P. S. Remington & Co., 1895.

Jeffrey, Francis, "Miss Edgeworth," (July 1809) *Contributions to the Edinburgh Review.* Vol. I; London: Longman, Browne, Green, and Longmans, 1853.

The Massachusetts Baptist Missionary Magazine. Vol. I; Boston: Manning and Loring, 1803.

Minutes of the General Assembly of the General Baptist Churches in England. W.T. Whitley, editor; Vol. II, 1731–1811; London: Kingsgate Press, 1910.

Minutes of the Philadelphia Baptist Association, from A.D., 1707 to A.D., 1807. A.D. Gillette, editor; Philadelphia: American Baptist Publication Society, 1851.

Pattison, Mark, "Tendencies of Religious Thought in England 1688–1750," *Essays and Reviews.* London: John W. Parker and Son, 1860.

Rippon, John, *The Baptist Annual Register.* Vols. I–IV; London, 1790–1802.

Scottish Journal of Theology. Vol. II, 1949; Vol. III, 1950; Edinburgh: Oliver & Boyd, Ltd.

Transactions of the Baptist Historical Society. Vols. VI–VII; London: Baptist Union Publication Department, 1918–1921. Then incorporated in *The Baptist Quarterly.*

UNPUBLISHED MATERIALS

Booth, Abraham, Four manuscript letters from the private collection of Dr. E.A. Payne, London.

de Visser, Peter, Manuscript letter regarding *The Reign of Grace*, 1949 American edition.

Minute Books, Four volumes, of the Little Prescott Street Baptist Church, now Church Hill Baptist Church, Walthamstow.

Newman, William, One manuscript letter from the private collection of Dr. E.A. Payne, London.

RAYMOND ARTHUR COPPENGER: A BIOGRAPHICAL SKETCH

In 1909, Raymond Arthur Coppenger was born at home in humble circumstances near the small town of Tellico Plains in the mountains of East Tennessee. As a child, he walked two miles along a dirt road to a one-room log school, but by his high school years, the family had moved to Atlanta, Georgia. While a student at Tech High, near Georgia Tech University, he worked in the railroad yards after class.

The fall after his graduation, he enrolled at Mercer University in Macon, Georgia, where he received his B.A. in English literature in 1933. Throughout his college years, he used his holidays to continue work in the rail yards of Atlanta, chiefly as a messenger. Sensing a call to ministry, he travelled to The Southern Baptist Theological Seminary in Louisville, Kentucky, from which he graduated with a Th.M. in 1936. While at Southern, he sang bass in the popular seminary quartet, which toured the South and appeared on programs of both the Southern and Northern Baptist Conventions in St. Louis 1936.

After seminary, he served as associate pastor of First Baptist Church, Newport, Tennessee, and then as pastor of churches in Butler, Tennessee, and Pennington Gap, Virginia. Butler was the only incorporated town inundated by a Tennessee Valley Authority reservoir, its residents relocated to high ground. He then accepted a position as director of Baptist student ministry at Auburn University in Alabama.

In the midst of World War II, he was commissioned a Naval chaplain and attended their school at the College of William and Mary in Virginia. After a tour of duty at a naval training centre near Detroit, where he met and married a University of Michigan graduate, Agnes Louise Crow, he received orders for a year's service in the Pacific, which took him from Pearl Harbour to Guadalcanal to China.

Returning to the U.S. after the war, he was Baptist student ministry director at the University of Kentucky, before heading to Edinburgh, Scotland, for doctoral studies under the G.I. Bill. Hugh Watt—who occupied one of the two chairs in Church History at the University of Edinburgh, was Principal of New College, and whose expertise was in the thought of Thomas Chalmers—was his principal professor. While in the United Kingdom, he also did summer work at Oxford University, where he and Agnes had the opportunity to hear a lecture by C.S. Lewis.

Back in the United States in 1947, he began teaching at Cumberland University in Lebanon, Tennessee, where he also served as first pastor of Immanuel Baptist Church. Subsequently, he taught philosophy and religion at Carson-Newman College in Jefferson City, Tennessee, Belmont College in Nashville, Tennessee, and Ouachita Baptist University in Arkadelphia, Arkansas. In the latter two appointments, he was the chairman of the department, and before his retirement, he was elected president of the southwest chapter of the Society for Biblical Literature.

In 1947, as Raymond and Agnes were leaving Edinburgh, they placed his dissertation notes in a railway locker, only to have them stolen. He was forced to reconstitute much of his research, and for this effort, Edinburgh allowed him to work under a British expatriate, Eric Rust, on the faculty of his alma mater, Southern Seminary. He also received significant guidance from E.A. Payne of Regent's Park College at Oxford, who was the doyen of English Baptist studies during the mid-twentieth century, and who also wrote a substantial article on Abraham Booth. Also helpful were the staff of Bristol Baptist College in England, Spurgeon's library at William-Jewell College in Liberty, Missouri, and the American Baptist Historical Society in Chester, Pennsylvania. His wife, Agnes, who typed the dissertation, was also a tremendous support in many ways. Finally, in 1953, he received the Ph.D. from Edinburgh for his work on Abraham Booth.

He and Agnes, who died in 2000, have three children, Susan, Anne, and Mark, the latter an apologetics professor at The Southern Baptist Theological Seminary in Louisville, Kentucky. Since Raymond was skilled in both construction and mechanics, the family lived in a house he had designed and built, and they rode in cars he renovated and maintained.

Throughout his college teaching years, Raymond continued post-doctoral studies—at George Washington University and the University of Colorado—led tour groups to Asia, the Middle East, and Europe, and served as a chaplain in the Naval Reserve, rising to the rank of lieutenant commander. An emeritus professor since 1974, Coppenger continues to supply-preach and joins in the ministry of his local church—and he does his best to keep up with his five grandchildren and five great-grandchildren!

www.ingramcontent.com/pod-product-compliance
Lightning Source LLC
Chambersburg PA
CBHW071955090426
42740CB00011B/1950